BEST CANADIAN POETRY 2026

GUEST EDITED BY MARY DALTON

SERIES EDITED BY ANITA LAHEY

BIBLIOASIS
WINDSOR, ONTARIO

FIRST EDITION
ISBN 978-1-77196-676-4 (Trade Paper)
ISBN 978-1-77196-677-1 (eBook)

Guest edited by Mary Dalton
Series edited by Anita Lahey
Editorial assistant: Ashley Van Elswyk
Copyedited by Emily Donaldson
Series designed and typeset by Ingrid Paulson

Published with the generous assistance of the Canada Council for the Arts, which last year invested $153 million to bring the arts to Canadians throughout the country, and the financial support of the Government of Canada. Biblioasis also acknowledges the support of the Ontario Arts Council (OAC), an agency of the Government of Ontario, which last year funded 1,709 individual artists and 1,078 organizations in 204 communities across Ontario, for a total of $52.1 million, and the contribution of the Government of Ontario through the Ontario Book Publishing Tax Credit and Ontario Creates.

PRINTED AND BOUND IN CANADA

CONTENTS

Anita Lahey

FOREWORD

Gifts of Uncertainty

It was language I loved, not meaning. I liked poetry better
when I wasn't sure what it meant.
—P. K. Page, "Something We Once Knew," *The New Quarterly*

Here's a definition like none you will find in the dictionary.

> *Clam* an old English word meaning to cramp
> fetter constrict or pinch as an iron
> clamp squeezes together so shellfish valves
> were seen to shut like a pair of pincers
> Clam also slang for dollar as in 5.

Read it aloud, as written, without the benefit of those pointedly absent commas. Feel the fettering constricting pinching as your mouth shapes the words, no breath, no pause to say *Wait stop not yet don't clam shut.* At the end of the stanza, that's just what happens: your mouth clams shut. On the words, on how you set the clamming in motion with your voice.

Here is another definition—two, actually—likewise situated outside the norms of an Oxford or Webster's. Each is accompanied by its own mouth, even before your own, the third, gets involved:

"Empathy is betrayal," said a mouth.
"Empathy is colonial," said another mouth.
Are there different mouths and faces?
Or do we have one big face?

There's a fourth mouth here. It belongs to the narrator, and utters not statements, but questions. This mouth belongs to someone who admits, in the stanza that follows, "The gift of certainty is not mine."

Welcome to the seventeenth annual edition of *Best Canadian Poetry*, an anthology that collects fifty poems by Canadian authors from among the thousand-plus that appeared in periodicals the previous calendar year. In the back of each edition, we print a list of up to fifty further notable poems, as well as the titles of the numerous print and online journals consulted by this year's guest editor. For this edition, your eye on the work of contemporary Canadian poets—and, by extension, the poetry chosen for publication by literary journal editors—is acclaimed Newfoundland poet Mary Dalton, who I'll introduce more fully below.

We also print brief commentaries by the authors on their poems, a popular part of this series that I highly recommend perusing. These aren't intended as explanations of the poems, rather as companion pieces that might reveal what spurred them, some related background, how their making unfolded. In their documentation of the thought processes, experimentations, revisions and even research efforts often undertaken by their authors, they tend to make for enlightening, often entertaining reading.

The excerpts I quoted above are from the first two poems in this year's anthology: "Clams," by John Reibetanz and "Checkpoint of the Mouth," by Ronna Bloom. (I am not referencing them in order; the anthology is alphabetized by title, and Bloom's poem appears first.) The "clams" in Reibetanz's poem represent grossly inadequate housing for workers and their families: "*little homes* thrown up / from boards shingles tarpapered fronts and roofs." Bloom's poem "speaks" about the inability to do just that in the face of unspeakable atrocities and a hotly politicized environment. She writes, "... No language is safe / Except dream language."

The hard substance of each poem is distressing. And yet, as you might have found while considering the lines above—especially if you tested them aloud—reading them offers a palpable, even potent, pleasure.

Is this a paradox? Maybe. Or maybe it's that poems affix language to reality: the right words, in the right order, as tried and retried until finally slotted—by texture, by pitch, by their faintest spice and fragrance—into place.

Let's give it a try.

In Reibetanz's "Clams," the rush and clang of that second line, with its crowded consonants and short sharp vowels—"fetter constrict or pinch"—grabs me as though by a hand thrust through the open window of a moving vehicle I must run to keep up with. Inevitably, I trip: over the slower beats of "iron" at the end of the line, landing hard on "clamp" down below. In comes "squeezes," which closes, like the top half of a clamshell, over the burning scrape in my knee. This breathless adventure carries on through the poem, line upon line, as if we're in some linguistic version of a car chase.

In Bloom's poem, the near-rhyme of the opposing viewpoints—empathy as "betrayal," empathy as "colonial"—brings the two sides of a war together in a kind of dance. They may not wish to take this turn about the ballroom together, they might purposely step on each other's toes (that rhyme is a little off), but they're held by those middle syllables gliding on their long vowels as if by an arm around a waist, then gracefully dipped, first one, then the other, into "yal" and "ial"—neither partner hitting the floor, nor letting go. Then the poem rights itself and spins off into questions, whirling until it's hard to recall who is who, which face belongs where.

In 2005, eminent Canadian poet P. K. Page wrote about how she fell in love with poetry for an occasional series on the topic in the Waterloo-based journal *The New Quarterly*. In her piece, she didn't speak of the important subjects poems may tackle, what they might have to teach or to say. She spoke of them as physical onslaught: "'Tyger, Tyger Burning Bright' and 'Kubla Kahn' crashed through me when I was about 10 or 12. I had no idea what either of them meant. I still don't know. Someone, I think it was AE (George Russell), said that metrics correspond to something in the soul."

Page's essay is collected in *TNQ*'s 2016 anthology *Falling in Love With Poetry*, and her report mirrors those of her companions in the book's pages. Ken Howe writes, of reading Tim Lilburn's *The Names of God*, "It was as if the words exploded in my face... It assaulted me, gouged my eyes." Bruce Taylor writes, of the nursery rhymes of Mother Goose, "...the beauty was in the sound of it; or rather, the saying of it, since the pleasure of these things is mainly in the mouth." Rae Crossman writes, of first reading a poem by Keats, "What? What? I read the lines over and over again. The words coming like slow, mighty waves crashing over me... The waves kept coming... The waves breaking over me, waves of words turning into tears. My god, I was crying. I was crying over a goddamn poem... I didn't even like poems." Patricia Young writes of different waves on what is, till they roll in, a desperately boring afternoon in 1965: "And then my fifth grade teacher is opening a book... I hear my teacher recite lines in which crashing waves are likened to white horses. I sit bolt upright because it's true!—their frothing bodies, their foamy tails lashing the air. As she continues to read, I can see waves bucking and hissing and throwing back their heads... In that moment, the classroom is not a classroom at all but a light-filled space in which a small miracle has occurred."

Some of you will be new to poetry, or new to its contemporary permutations. You may know Chaucer, Rumi, Shakespeare, Plath. Your acquaintance with verse might begin and end with Mother Goose. Others of you will be well-steeped in verse and its tricks. Metaphor mindful, slant-rhyme-wise. Poets, reviewers, teachers, scholars, with your academic interests, your aesthetic leanings, stylistic or political concerns, your established tastes. No matter where you land on this spectrum, here is how I would entreat you to make your way through this anthology: as unknowingly as you can, letting the words, lines, sounds and rhythms, as Page put it, "crash" through you.

Be curious about the arrangement of words and their effects, the sounds they make in your ear, the shapes they form in your mouth. Allow yourself to be drawn or charmed by a phrase, though you can't immediately parse it or defend its being there at all. Does a moment seem indulgent, overblown? Too bland, obvious, naïve, cynical, sweet, obtuse? Don't dismiss it right off. Every reader won't love every poem here, and not every poem dazzles (or "crashes") on first acquaintance. Some poems are shy; some so grounded as to seem plain; some patterned with such quiet inevitability that their hum might be missed.

Trust this: The poems here are not fly-by-nights. They deal in profound, serious matters of human existence—war, the climate crisis, the legacies of injustice, whose histories matter to whom, yearning, regret, love, illness, grief, immigrant life, ageing, garbage, storks, ashes, real estate, the death of trees.

So, all this. Yes, sure. But the chosen words first. Tongue against teeth, rounded lips. How they melt on your tongue, tumble down your throat and balloon in your chest. How they start—airily or with a pop, easing in or at full gallop. And how they end: backed against a wall, on a sigh, staring somewhere off to your right. When a poem matches clean, clear language to something out here, in the world—whether that something is horrific or delightful—it offers to readers a rare and simple satisfaction. It makes sense. I don't necessarily mean conscious, or describable sense. I mean a "sense" that resides in the body, in the mouth.

This is a feat that belongs wholly to poetry. It's a phenomenon that I will call appropriate utterance. The called-for words, somehow found, then arranged, by the poet, in the most rewarding order, can bring on, not the certainty that the speaker in Bloom's poem confesses she lacks, but more like a rush of relief. A tightly knotted muscle softens; blood and oxygen pour in.

*

We deliberately seek guest editors for *Best Canadian Poetry* who not only write poetry themselves but who engage with the craft in other ways: who have actively joined in the ongoing conversation in, around, and about Canadian poetry. These are people who, to some extent, think and breathe poetry; who live their lives on the line.

Enter this year's guest editor, celebrated Newfoundland poet Mary Dalton. Author, critic, professor, and essayist, Dalton is known for the wit, humour, and nervy vernacular that drives her own verse (if you want a crash course in Newfoundland English, read Dalton). She's a past editor of the interdisciplinary journal *Newfoundland Studies*, edited and co-published the literary journal *TickleAce* for several years, and founded the SPARKS literary festival at Memorial University of Newfoundland.

As a poet, she plays boldly with forms, from the riddle to the cento. Her poems teem with people who seem as if they've just hauled themselves up a steep, winding road, pounded by sleet, with a tale burning their tongues, and the hope that you'll ask to hear it. Her most recent collection, published in 2024, is *Interrobang*—named, appropriately, after the joint question mark and exclamation mark, as in, "Huh?!" She calls this symbol, in her poem "Punctuation Marks," the "prince of ambivalence." The "prince's" emphatic bewilderment suits the lively voices that populate her verse (or how it feels to encounter them). Here's her character Alba, facing off with a realtor in "Luck." Pity the realtor, who's for sure got her hands full with this one:

Sure my duck I grew up
with those cursed wild roses,
worse than the dandelions if
you're wanting a garden—
roots down to hell
with side roots to purgatory.
Knock a few thousand off
and I'll take on a rose-fight.

A reader needn't spend much time with Dalton's work to glean the depth of her respect for everyday speech, and her ability to score it. Here, for example, are the first notes of "Taxi Dispatcher Jazz" from her 2006 collection *Red Ledger*: "Where you at, five five? / Where you headed at? / Picking up a job are ya?" In an interview with the poet Barbara Nickel in 2002, Dalton said, "For as long as I can remember, speech rhythms have fascinated me. When I was five or six, an Irish policeman dropped into our house to ask for directions. I was ravished by what I described to myself as the ripply sound of his voice...."

My own introduction to Dalton's verse was through *Merrybegot*, published in 2003 by Véhicule Press. I was hooked from the opening of "After All That," the first poem in the book:

Gumption? It's clear he didn't
Have the sense God gave a kitten.
And it was after all that
He got in tack with the other one—
A real blatherskite
If I ever saw one...

A fierce bit of finger-wagging over a mug of strong tea, it's all over in eleven quick lines—four breaths, if that. And: "blatherskite." There's a word to stuff in your pocket for later. Dalton's poetry is rife with such treasures; reading her work's like skimming the shore for bits of sea-polished glass on an especially lucky low tide.

"Flirrup," also from *Merrybegot*, is one of my favourite Dalton poems. It bobs like a nursery rhyme, but, like many such seemingly light compositions, it's perfectly chilling: "Fairy squalls on the water. / I'm marooned at the window, / Waiting for the fog man, / Sewing the old black veil."

When you consider the hints—water, fog, the window (with her at it), ominous veil—the anxiety thrumming in these tight, four-beat lines becomes logical. But it's already under your skin before you stop to figure out why. To offer one small example of what's sensorially at play, you're "marooned" by the very way that word moves. Reading the poem is to be lashed by its "squalls" of foreboding before understanding what they are.

In an essay on contemporary poetry in Newfoundland (originally a talk) that appears in her book, *Edge: Essays, Reviews, Interviews*, Dalton laments the lack of due credit given to poetry as a salient cultural offering. "Poets in their achieved poems have something of much value to offer. They are muzzled by certain assumptions that have gained wide currency and are almost daily confirmed by the more mindless practitioners of journalism. One assumption is that poems are exclusively containers of little private feelings, about one's cat, or a certain light in the sky. Poems are small amusements, for small minds. Thus the lightly teasing remarks of one of my colleagues, passing in the hallway last week, 'Are the poets writing about spring in winter these days?'"

Not exactly, Dalton may have retorted. Here is a taste of her own seasonal poetry, in "Janneying": "Every winter it was the same racket. / A hint of the janneying, our mother'd / Have copper kittens, but after a bit / She'd give in to us, say yes we could go."

How about the moon? Are poets writing about the moon, still? Dalton is. In a way. It appears in *Merrybegot*'s title poem (look it up, by the way; the meaning of that distinctly regional compound word will click marvellously into place): "When the moon was newing and the night burnt black, / Some rapscallion, some young pelt, some nuzzle-tripe / Set off down the path with the go of a born-again preacher…"

In her talk, Dalton was speaking directly of poetry in Newfoundland, but her complaint is relevant nationwide, as is her defence of what poets bring the table: "…for poetry is embedded in the language in which it is written, in cadence. Poetry is what gets lost in translation. Poetry is a place to stand, to speak *yes* to the particularities of a people's existence, to awaken an awareness of and a respect for every tradition; thus it may lead to a healthier ecology of Canadian cultures than we have now."

The sensitivity of the ear that Dalton brings to the year in Canadian poetry cannot be overstated: her penchant for vivid, inventive talk; her appreciation of a clean—or deliberately offbeat—rhythm; her belief in the intrinsic value of such pleasures. The poems to follow found in Dalton a reader who knows a voice when she hears one, a reader who appreciates a good old, head-clearing, home-brewed line, and who'll bravely drink it down. Her selections are testament to her lifelong habit of listening, which she has paired with an equally devoted fascination with poetry's wiles and forms. They demonstrate a deep-seated faith in the poem's hard, glittering *something*ness. Its soundings and its mattering.

Anita Lahey
Ottawa, Ontario, unceded
Algonquin Anishinabek territory
June 2025

Mary Dalton

INTRODUCTION

The Anthologist as Star-Nosed Mole

Then I got into the poem—
it doesn't matter which poem—
and let it take me
wherever it was going.
—Kayla Czaga, "Dad Poem"

meet me at the buttes. the dust & ink mixed together
with blood.
blood is what makes this real. listen to *naahsa* (grandma):
'make everything a gift with words.'
—Henry Heavyshield, "Storytelling for Young Warriors"

My heart rouses
thinking to bring you news
of something
that concerns you
and concerns many men....
—William Carlos Williams, "Asphodel, That Greeny Flower"

Dear Reader, in making your star-nosed way through this anthology, looking for "something written" (to echo the ideal reader of M. W. Miller's poem), you will likely make observations and linkages other than my own. Think of the following account as one side of a conversation with you. Reading anthologies myself over the years I've developed a habit of leaping headlong into the works assembled; afterwards I settle comfortably into the introduction, eager to engage with the anthologist's commentary, aware that it might send me back to the poems with some new questions, or some new perspective. Maybe that method will work for you, too?

*

Let me tell you about the star-nosed mole. It's a curious creature, one I've come to associate with the process of searching out the energies pulsing in a genuine poem, whether one is maker or reader. The star-nosed mole spends most of its time in damp underground tunnels. It goes by touching, feeling its way along, navigating by means of the twenty-two fleshy tentacles (the star) at the end of its snout. Those tentacles have over 100,000 nerve fibres; the star-nosed mole has the most sensitive touch organs of any known mammal. Its nose has been called "the nose that sees." Constantly on the move in its search for food, it is a voracious eater, needing to consume 50 percent of its body weight every day. According to *The Guinness Book of Records*, it is, among the mammals, the fastest eater on earth.

There's a headlong, unwilled quality to the activity of the star-nosed mole, a blind searching quality that seems to me akin to the energies operating in the creating of a poem, as well as in the process of discovery involved in reading a good poem. When Dennis Lee, in his essay "Cadence, Country, Silence," gives the name *cadence* to the particular aspect of poetry which he tries to summon forth, he is attempting to describe something similar:

> I speak of "hearing" cadence, but the sensation isn't auditory. It's more like sensing a constantly changing tremor with your body: a play of movement and stress, torsion and flex—as with the kinaesthetic perception of the muscles.

In my reading for *Best Canadian Poetry 2026* I quested like the star-nosed mole, snout aquiver for the vital pulse. I aimed to read without program, without preference for particular poetics, region, gender, age, or ethnicity—not with the territorial sweep of the eye but sniffing and snuffling along for the spoor of the genuine.

There were certain touchstones, such as Edward Hirsch's observation that "the lyric poem exists somewhere in the region—the register—between speech and song." As well, the myriad manners in which form may fuse with content became apparent in the course of my explorations. The poems which distinguished themselves drew in a variety of ways upon the range of resources available to the poet: among them line- and stanza-shaping, image, figure, and voice.

There is, of course, a variety of themes and types of poems. Some of the types and techniques to be found are: ghazal; ode; monologue; catalogue poems, prose poems; dream narratives; pieces inspired by diary format and online comments format; pieces drawing on vernacular and dialogue. A surreal element operates in several poems, as does humour, often of a wryly ironic sort. The dominant mode is free verse, with its music derived from chains of consonance and assonance. In some instances, anaphora drives the rhythm. The couplet, that wily stanza with its capacity to evoke now confinement and now a ramped-up surging energy, is a frequent structural device.

At this point, looking back over the terrain of the gathering I've made, I'm feeling my way among the poems once again, in a mole-like sensing of the contours of the collection—and recognizing again the truth of Adam Sol's observation, made in his *How A Poem Moves: A Field Guide for Readers of Poetry*, that this is a golden age for the art of poetry. More of Sol's assertion later—first I'd like to sketch some of the ways in which the poems of *Best Canadian Poetry 2026* reflect the society within which they exist.

The reader of this anthology will hear within a community of many voices. The poems explore contemporary experiences of Indigenous people in Jennifer Gossoo's portrait of her grandmother, "Nôhkom," and in Conor Kerr's sardonic account of the dilemmas of "Fancy University Boy." They delve into the dislocations and longings of those who have come to Canada from other cultures or whose roots lie in other cultures—in, say, Vivek Sharma's dialogue of "shifting places," "Imaginary Breakfast with Real People;" in Nofel's hymn to the beauty and comfort of the Arabic language in his ghazal "In Arabic"; and in Khashayar "Kess" Mohammadi's haunting "Uber-Eats Ghazal." Some of the poems focus on people Othered by virtue of their economic status, their ethnicity, age, their gender identity, or their language, or by illness of body or mind. There are poems focusing on the relations between generations, as in Susan White's "Some Late for Them to Be at the Fish" and Glenn Hayes' "It Is Not Heart to Essay"; the sorrow of those haunted by history, its past horrors, as in Emily Kedar's "Yellow Felt Stars" and Kevin Irie's "How to Pack for Internment (150 Pounds)," and by current conflicts—all, all are reflected here in poems which first and foremost have found their places in the anthology because of their being snuffled out, rooted into, by the mole anthologist intent upon their living energies *as poems.* These poems are not programmatic; they often embody ambivalences, complexes of feeling. "I am just a stand-alone question mark—," says Ronna Bloom's speaker in "Checkpoint of the Mouth," a poem full of dashes and question marks. All the poems make their own music; all bespeak the tangled emotions of individuals caught in the toils of time and culture. They bring us the news which humans desperately need and which, as William Carlos Williams maintains in "Asphodel, That Greeny Flower," poems, unlike journalism, can offer. They range among voices and tonalities, topographies and geographies, among nations and time periods. They take inspiration from various ways of knowing, including science (most notably in Sylvia LeGris' "In the Wake of" and Paul Moorehead's "Requirement Galore").

The poems in this book were selected from those published in Canadian print or online journals by Canadian (or Canada-based) poets. Given editorial and publishing timelines, it's likely that many of the poems considered were written and submitted during the pandemic, a time of general uncertainty and overarching threat. Nonetheless, there is an element of the jeremiad about the anthology which is not entirely attributable to the pandemic alone. The titular character in Irina Dumitrescu's "Criseyde" links herself with Cassandra and then gives voice to her sense of being unheard: "I am used by now / To my voice getting caught in my teeth. / It doesn't help / That I can smell tomorrow's burning." Patricia Young's sinister vignette "The Thing with the Wings" calls to mind Yeats' rough beast, slouching towards Bethlehem to be born. Darrell Epp's surreal "That's Not a Piñata, That's a Hornets' Nest" depicts an addled world, a vast meaningless circus, fusing images of planetary degradation with language of war and online commerce. In "Darwin Awards Song," an ironic ode celebrating two drunken teens who fall to their deaths after copulating while perched on a balcony railing, John Wall Barger casts a scornful eye on a dystopian society unmoored from all care for community and all restraint: "From birth we advised: / keep your things close, do not share, /   it's yours, all yours." Some poems express the struggle to defy gravity obliquely. Sue Sinclair's speaker in "Pfeilstorch" gazes at the taxidermied body of an "arrow stork," one of many storks that overwinter in Africa, then fly back to Europe with the arrows still in their bodies. She feels a sense of communion with the wounded bird: "... I know I can stare into your glass eye in a way that most / animals won't tolerate. I know what pain looks like when it's gone."

America looms as a site of dysfunction and decline in certain poems. Evelyn Lau's "Cursing, Flailing," a record of a post-pandemic road-trip across that country, paints a dystopian portrait of a nation wrapped in plastic, riddled with fear of nuclear war—a nation of tent cities, trailer parks, and bars, and, everywhere, chemical-laden food. The sound of the ocean is a "painful roar, the sound / of a million creatures dying." Shane Neilson's "How to lose the audience" is another dark vision of America, a wittily vigorous indictment of "the extinguishing empire, in terminal decline," by a disaffected academic experiencing his own off-meds decline. Both these poems share a characteristic attributed to poems in general: they are news that stays news. But it has to be said that they seem particularly prescient at the moment, as does Nicholas Bradley's wry missive "To the Border Agent Who Confiscated My Book of Poetry." A spoofing of unreasonable customs regulations, it also makes a sly case for poetry.

War and economic upheaval figure among the poets' thematic concerns. Some of the poems between these covers consider the far-reaching effects of war in Ukraine, among them Erin Moure's "Flourish" and John O'Neill's "The News." Some engage with the Israel-Palestine conflict from various perspectives, as in Ronna Bloom's "Checkpoint of the Mouth" and Ozayr Saloojee's "The Little Things." Some confront economic injustice as played out in matters of housing past and present: in John Reibetanz's "Clams," Karen Solie's "Prime Location," and Dave Hickey's "Real Estate Sign."

Many poems invite the reader to consider the havoc being wreaked upon our planet. Ariel Gordon's catalogue poem, "A mudlarker's diary," and Sue Goyette's "from *Monoculture: A commentary of monologues*" both focus on nature beleaguered, by plastic in the diary poem and by the relegation of a forest to a kind of museum display in Goyette's poem. Goyette's is a darkly comic imagining of the visitors' reviews of the entertainment they've been offered, as might be found in a guestbook or in online comments pages. Nancy Huggett's "We're Doubling Down, Says Darren Woods" creates a scene of apocalypse in response to Exxon's CEO saying, in 2023, that his firm is "doubling down" on their extraction of fossil fuels: "We've doubled down / restocked the pile that feeds / the flames that drive the heat / that burns the world around us / while we sleep." Sylvia Legris' "In the Wake of," a taut poem linking lungs—the planet's and ours—creates a deep unease by drawing on the scientific and the oracular in its lines. Danielle Devereaux tackles the subject (among others) in her witty poem "Lending Library, Heaven." There's quite a to-do when Rachel Carson's *Silent Spring* is returned to Heaven's library with pages missing—turns out it was mutilated by Hitchcock. He confesses to Jesus, the head archivist: "... It's that first chapter. The one where no birds / sing. Christ, I just can't get enough of it."

The poems described above give some idea of the extent to which the poems in this anthology warrant attention as part of the broader public discourse about the current state of the world. While a sense of general threat emerges from these particular poems, in many others the intimate experience of the individual is foregrounded. Some are preoccupied with smaller social units—a family, say, or a father-daughter relationship, as in Jaeyun Yoo's moving tribute, "have you seen my father." The poem invites the reader to truly see an immigrant father, to recognize his humanity and the diminished quality of his life in his new country. The poem is at once a portrait of one father and of Everyfather. The daughter has, she says, "learned grace in grief." The reverie closes with the poignant question, "have you seen my father / carry city lights on his glasses / as he sleeps on the midnight bus." Love and sorrow are also mingled in Susan White's "Some Late for Them to Be at the Fish," an account of how a granddaughter navigates with compassion the mental wanderings of her grandmother, whose morphine has her "lost in memory." Another grandmother appears in Jennifer Gossoo's "Nôhkom," a figure revered by her granddaughter for her knowledge, wisdom, courage, and strength under pressure. Glenn Hayes' "It Is Not Heart to Essay" is a nephew's meditative account of what is lost and what remains—his ability to communicate by singing—when his aunt's speech is scrambled by a stroke. Craig Francis Power's hard-edged vision of St. John's in "Walking My Three-Year-Old to Nanny's Place, Easter

Sunday 2017" is leavened by his daughter's refrain; even as a site of grim ironies, the poem deftly gestures at redemption, a transforming love, the innocence of a child. The suffering figure in Kayla Czaga's poem "Painkiller" is a daughter haunted by her father's death; the poem is a surreal litany of her (futile) efforts to be rid of his ashes.

Some poems explore the trauma of a single figure, as in Puneet Dutt's brief internal monologue "Lucky," which dramatizes a woman's cascade of thoughts about childbearing, risk, and loss. One of the most wrenching poems in the collection, Cassandra Myers' prose triptych "Squeal," links the brutal violation of rape and the terror of animals corralled for slaughter. In "Surfacing, Copenhagen Harbour," Carolina Corcoran's mermaid ironically reports the violence she must visit on herself to meet the prince's standards, involving "tale-bifurcation and a pair / of high heels...." The mermaid becomes a figure of all the Othered who are denied "soul-status": "Getting a soul is big business especially / among us half-breeds. We queued for hours, / centaurs satyrs manticores minotaurs...." In "Some Questions," a catalogue piece at once comic and horrific, Megan Morrison presents a woman's constant interrogation of self; above all she wants to fit in, to be good, to do well. And Petra Chambers maps the land of anxiety in a more comic vein in "My answer to the question 'how are you?' at the grocery store."

Humour figures as well in certain poems which explore the power of imagination to transform limiting circumstances. In "Gay Messiah," Estlin McPhee conjures up "other queers" by means of witchcraft to create in their small town a "party in [their] mind." Among the guests is Jesus, who plays emo songs and looks like Rufus Wainwright. The tone is wry, but ultimately the poem is about redemption. "Yoo-Hoo" by Misha Solomon is also about a party in the mind, this time a party of two. The speaker engages in a stream of yearning, whimsical chatter directed in his mind to someone he notices on a cafe patio. The whole poem is one wistful yoo-hoo, but he never utters a word. In her playful "Ode to Joy," Erin Wilson's speaker apostrophizes the items in her kitchen, rejoicing in their presence ("Oven, philosopher friend. // Clock, most enduring brother"). The poem recognizes that the kitchen party is on one level an escape from the shadow of the news, but embraces the domestic, the immediate, as an imaginative countering of what's beyond that refuge. The need is to "escape reality / to enter reality."

The finding of solace and meaning in the moment, in an embracing of the existential, is a feature of a group of poems in this collection linking the imagination and water. Richard Greene's "On the Use of the Sextant" describes the navigation by dead reckoning of sailors in "their wooden boats of spirit," moving "in the ocean of things as they obscurely are." The cadence of the poem is itself an affirmation of mind moving in a measured, considered way. In A. F. Moritz's "Quibble with Hegel" the perfection of the moment and the transforming power of imagination are embodied in the image of an acorn cap becoming "a little coracle bound for mystic Ireland" in the play of children "kneeling by water." George Moore, in "Local Fishermen," conveys, through image and the lapping rhythms of his couplets, the harmony of movement of fishers and sea: "the wind and the water and these men / must be doing something always going." Michael Ondaatje's "Lock" muses upon time, aging, moving toward death, and the power of poetry to carry one in memory, just as an open lock enables a canoe to move to another part of a river. Water, poetry, change, the unknown—the poem, clear-eyed, accepts the moving along the river. Steve McOrmond's site of transforming imagination is a formidable ocean. In "The Science of Skipping Stones" he evokes the seeming magic of making stones dance across its water: "When the lift is strong enough, it propels / the rock up into the air again and again." Eventually the stone is "pinballing into the cosmos // The sky darkens by gradations. Pixel by pixel, / the star chart blinks into being."

Throughout the anthology the poems themselves, even the darkest ones, are expressive of a triumph of the human spirit, for the shaping of art in the direst circumstances involves the transformation of pain through the medium of language. However, the water poems linked above operate directly as poems of consolation, highlighting moments of flight, of being at home in the universe.

The poems gathered here, and those listed also as worthy of note, are one strong sign of the flourishing of poetry in our time. There are many others. There's a cornucopia of print and online literary journals across Canada. The Canada Council and provincial arts bodies support many of them. Books of poetry published within a year hover around 150; funding agencies foster this activity also. Creative writing programs are thriving in universities. Poetry prizes abound. And there is certainly no shortage of fine poetry. As the anthology you're holding demonstrates (along with its predecessors in this Best Canadian Poetry series, on the go since 2008), Canadian poets are engaging with the world around them and making compelling art in the process. But is this truly a golden age of poetry if the institutions that might be expected to carry the poet's voice beyond coteries to the general public fail to do so? Consider how infrequently (an understatement, that!) volumes of poetry are reviewed in our national newspapers. Consider the amount of coverage on CBC. When poets appear in the book pages of our biggest newspapers or on our CBC book programs it's frequently because they've brought out a novel or a memoir. How often does a book of poems or a poetry anthology appear in newspaper seasonal lists of Best Books? Do public libraries feature poetry in their occasional Best Of columns?

What are the causes of this neglect? Certain assumptions seem to have gained wide currency since the 1970s, when poetry flourished in the public sphere. One is that contemporary poetry is utterly obscure, a thicket far too impenetrable for the ordinary mortal. In his essay "Obscurity and the Poet," Randall Jarrell observes the irony of such a stance:

> [The poet of our time] has inherited a situation in which no one looks at him and in which, consequently, everyone complains that he is invisible: for that corner into which no one looks is always dark. And people who have inherited the custom of not reading poets justify it by referring to the obscurity of the poems they have never read....

What can we as poets and readers of poetry do to make poetry visible beyond poetry circles? "Can Poetry Matter?" (an online essay written by poet Dana Gioia some time ago for *The Atlantic*) offers a list of suggestions which are still current. An essay of mine about the Newfoundland context appears in a miscellany of my prose, *Edge*, published by Palimpsest. It's my hope that the book you're holding may prompt you, each in your own way, to make the outstanding writing of Canadian poets more visible in our culture.

Mary Dalton
St. John's, Newfoundland
June 2025

Ronna Bloom

CHECKPOINT OF THE MOUTH

Before even the door is—
It is shut.
To dare~~speak.~~

I stepped into—then out of—the family
toasting *chayalim* at the *bris*. Invoking soldiers
at a celebration of birth pokes a gun
at life. In biblical Hebrew. No language is safe.
Except dream language.

And then I think: Palestine?
But who am I to speak any word?
Speaker (it) matters.

I am just a standalone question mark—

Not even God—if there was, is—
would be permissible aloud.

Love is my inside voice.
Shame travels freely but gets me nowhere.
The silence of my mouth
does not speak for the rest of me

For a world celebrating the non-binary,
we've gone pretty either/or.

Eventually these words sphincter out.

Thank you, she said, they said,
for being Jewish in public. I panicked.

"Empathy is betrayal," said a mouth.
"Empathy is colonial," said another mouth.
Are there different mouths and faces?
Or do we have one big face?

The gift of certainty is not mine.
I bowed inside. I stood up straight.

—from *Queen's Quarterly*

John Reibetanz

CLAMS

"We have 500 people coming in here and paying their $5 each every month now," said Mr. W. S. Dinnick, the manager of the Standard Loan Company. "This plan has solved the problem of the workingmen's houses . . . . They were all as happy as clams in their little homes."

—*The Toronto Star*, 1907

Clam an Old English word meaning cramp
fetter constrict or pinch as an iron
clamp squeezes together so shellfish valves
were seen to shut like a pair of pincers
Clam also slang for dollar as in 5.

Some of the lots were only ten feet wide
none had water mains sewers or drains no
paved roads or sidewalks *little homes* thrown up
from boards shingles tarpapered fronts and roofs
by crews of neighbours in house-building "bees."

All happy through summer and into fall
playing soccer on the flats picnicking
on the heights picking berries in ravines
refugees from Europe's crowded slumlands
out from under shadowing tenements.

Winter gifted them with unemployment
last-hired immigrants first to be fired
a struggle to keep every $5
from being spirited off by cold winds
that carried whimpers of hungry children.

Ice on the walls of the bedrooms drove them
into the kitchen to sleep on the four
beneath the iron mouth of a woodstove
fed with bits of coal the children picked up
along the railway tracks where passing trains

sometimes picked off slower-moving children
and when the coal ran out they fed the stove
scrap lumber furniture bedroom floorboards
bone waste from Sunday dinner roasts scraped clean
clam shells scavenged from affluent garbage.

—from *The Fiddlehead*

Irina Dumitrescu

CRISEYDE

They said Cassandra
Was the cursed one
But every woman knows too much.
I am used by now
To my voice getting caught in my teeth.
It doesn't help
That I can smell tomorrow's burning.
No one is interested
In the geometry
Of a falling city.
I sit politely and fan myself
Listening to old philosophies
Trying not to show
I see the sparks of death in their eyes.
My soles feel the road to come
The cool boards of an enemy's ship
The freedom of early surrender.

—from the *Times Literary Supplement*

Evelyn Lau

CURSING, FLAILING

The world is on the brink of nuclear war,
says a voice on the radio, near the border
between Oregon and California. Our first road trip
post-pandemic, and motel rooms groan with cold
even as plum blossoms line the freeway. In America
food mashes into sweet pablum
against the roofs of our mouths—

a stir of chemicals and enriched flour, pre-digested.
Ding-Dongs shaped like hockey pucks, corn chips
pushed through an extruder. 99 cents for a cup
of soda swill, small or X-large, so I cradle
a bucket-sized container of pop in my lap,
docile as a doped baby. Thanks to COVID
every plastic item comes wrapped in an extra film

of plastic, and turd-coloured rooms reek
of hospital-grade disinfectant. Praise to plastic straws
instead of paper tubes that disintegrate
in carbonation, leaving mush to slurp up!
Praise to the gleam of plastic cutlery,
its utility and malleability, its future journey adrift
for decades through miraculous oceans!
We unwrap burgers the size of our heads

while parked beside a tent city, gnaw gritty patties,
lick sauce dispensed in measured dollops.
On a beach between San Francisco and Santa Cruz
I crawl into a lean to built by a homeless man
who will reclaim it at sunset. Will bombs
find us here? Only the ocean's painful roar, the sound
of a million creatures dying. It seems a crime

to walk in America, the few pedestrians
stumbling out of trailer parks and bars
scanning for trouble and cursing, flailing.
The motel lobby sign says there's a $100 fine
for using hair dye—it ruins the towels—
but *everyone*, the clerk says, *wants to change*
their identity. Young women pass me in the halls,
hoodies up, PJ bottoms flapping, slippers slapping.
I squat on a curb by the entrance—COVID stacked away
the lobby chairs—and guests ask, *Ma'am, do you work here?*

—from *Geist*

John Wall Barger

DARWIN AWARDS SONG

Let us celebrate you,
Anastasia and Miguel, copulating on a balcony,
falling eight storeys.

From birth we advised:
keep your things close, do not share,
it's yours, all yours.

We were fools. Perhaps now
you are rocks falling into an abyss
for one hundred years.

Does it matter? Now all you had
is impounded. As if it were never yours!
Even the memories,

even the last: his erection in the dark.
Even your unpaid parking tickets.
Even those crates

of unread books in your parents' attic.
Even the possum in your garden
you never mentioned to anyone.

We're all teenagers, stoned,
horny, stepping out of the party. Praise us all!
Cut loose our strings.

We told you *we* were the teachers, *this*
the class. It's all for the good, we said,
hoping you would make it so.

Now look what happened:
you're no longer invited to dinner.
Even the good feeling

you became the wall around. Miguel
hoisted Anastasia onto the railing.
Anastasia unzipped him.

Let us giggle with them.
Let us make love to the air.
Like a Godard jump-cut.

Trick of bad editing.
That sound? A phone ringing.
Yes, it sounds close. It's not.

—from *EVENT*

Conor Kerr

FANCY UNIVERSITY BOY

Aho
Fancy university boy, wears a collared shirt, distinguished.
Cheque came in from Rupertsland and he's gonna buy
Some textbook that costs about a quarter of what he paid
For his truck. White guy wrote it but acknowledges unceded
Territory but not Treaty where he's gonna read it.
Fancy university boy's embarrassed about the truck he parks
At a friend's auntie's place. She's a prof at the school.
Gave her a bunch of moose that Buddy and him hunted up
Last fall. Auntie Prof is happy because she gives it out to
All the students who need something to eat and there's a
Lot of them. Fancy university boy wants to do something
Like that but he doesn't know jack shit about talking to
People and he doesn't know jack shit about how to be a
White guy and he doesn't know jack shit about how to do
Good in school. He used to get the highest grades back in
The town school, but that was just because he could read
And no one else could so the teachers who drove in from
The city on the daily said "ahh fuck it someone has to get
An A may as well be fancy university boy." And he got the A
And he still doesn't know jack shit. But that's about to change
When he gets this textbook and he swears that he's gonna
Read this one. He's gonna get invited to a fancy party where

People are gonna notice his collared shirt and he's not gonna
Say gonna, he'll say going to. And no one will comment on his
NDN accent. Every day he practices saying his "G's" and turning
"D's" into "T's." It'll come and he won't have to go home and
He'll move to the southside, date white women, read the textbook.

—from *The Fiddlehead*

Erín Moure

FLOURISH (MAY 2022)

To always bear this certain tension
An inheritance
An interstice
Melody
It comes from my mother
she was born in lands of Ukraine
she was ever a resistant
she knew how to disappear
how to fully vanish
leaving no residue
but wind and snow

Into *me* she
has vanished
every day she gets up washes her
face vanishes
walking the full length of the kitchen on
the wind into the snow
My face wet
I wipe it with my forearm
"use a towel" she says from inside me
"mom there is none in this snow"
:
:

I see her again this very morning
perched on a branch outside where should be birds
When I visited her then in ancient Calgary
(ancient because before the war)
she wanted me to make my coffee first
so she could make hers with just the residue
in case of bombings
that alter the terrain
so that it cannot be thereafter mediated or even known
Bombs upend the earth
artifice where love is no
co-incidence
Знову зацвіте українська земля *Ukrainian land will blossom again*

She is now (my mother) no bigger than a bird
small and fluffed
brown and grey
When dead for fifteen years it happens
you start vanishing slowly from the world *La terre ukrainienne refleurira*
its periscopes
its holograms
its scapulae and palettes
your feathers
tiny
indecent partisans of the snows
Still audible yes oh yes
as birdsong
berries grasses

as a hardiness
as blossoms
roots
in me as residue
she endures and is still speaking

(Ukraine will flourish)

—from *carte blanche*

Estlin McPhee

GAY MESSIAH

We all have our little rebellions. I, for instance,
cut off my hair and take up witchcraft,

will chant anything sublunary
or otherwise to summon other queers

to my small town. Primarily they materialize
from old books, their outlines smudgy,

their clothing outdated. Resurrected
and exhausted, they are busy

with their own dramas and don't want to talk
to me. Shakespeare is here, mingling

with Artemis, who won't stop fiddling
with her arrows. Turns out even the godliest

among us has something to prove
to their parents. At the party

in my mind, I'm in charge for once,
so Jesus is here, is queer,

and looks eerily similar
to Rufus Wainwright. He slouches

at the piano, playing songs
he learned from the dead.

Emo, yes, but you work with what you've got.
I sit on the thick carpet in my brother's

hand-me-downs and sing along, entranced
by the new outline of my skull,

that lightness like a halo. By midnight
we're all holding hands, flesh

and ghost. Jesus brings out a cauldron,
travel-size, and lights up

a fire in it, tells us to burn
what no longer serves us.

Where to start? I turn out my pockets.
And will I have anything

left after? Jesus stops in front of me.
Your turn, he says. My turn.

—from *EVENT*

Jueyun Yoo

HAVE YOU SEEN MY FATHER

walk home past the Han River?
        paisley tie tight as a soda cap
after twelve hours trading stocks
        belly-deep bows
to grey men twirling fountain pens.
        have you seen the ashtray grow
into an ant hill, my father spins
        round and round, a rain of layoffs.
hope hides in a weathervane
        pointing across the East Sea
and never did I learn how to say goodbye
        other than my father and grandfather
chain-smoking at the airport parking lot.

have you seen my father ring ring ring
        onions, condoms and gum
at Save-On-Foods, or have you
        unseen my father, playing tetris
with udon bowls and chopsticks
        a dishwasher at some sushi joint.
bank statements are coasters
        for rice wine, each spill
blurs the ink, blackens his thumb.
        he sits under the starry glow

of slot machines, pulls the lever
        again and again
as if loosening a fire hydrant
        and he is a burning house.

        I have seen how
autumn is mourned by a leaf
        gently pressed inside a book
and learned grace in grief—
        have you seen my father
carry city lights on his glasses
        as he sleeps on the midnight bus.

—from *The Fiddlehead*

Shane Neilson

HOW TO LOSE THE AUDIENCE

I am, of course, not taking my medication. Seven days,
I think? Long enough to be in terminal decline. Lowell
once wrote of a bullshit "monotonous sublime" but when
I wake these Sunday mornings, I'm no chinook breaking
loose, but rather the beers Cash had for breakfast on his way
to dessert. The last dessert I had was as a child—or when
treated as a child, in carceral hospital. Key lime pie. Key
lime pie on stainless steel. They say this place is Missouri.
A conference, at a sub-state university, and yet money is vast,
classic American cock projection, mid-century stalwart brick
and walkable spread. Even the pitiable schools hereabouts
are richer than the ones that had me. I come from ratty stands
and rusted, bent chainlink folded into pleats by vandals.
This isn't coming out right; I could do better if the thoughts
were clear and bright as the sun was over O'Hare and Decatur.
Here in Joplin, Missouri, the leaves are still green. Still! Back
home, the trees turncoated a month and a half ago, girding
themselves. Terminal decline. Freefall. Wind feels good
around the ears, but I don't recommend this for the folks
at home. Something irritating me: how people's pasts
are used as weapons. Didn't this place have a revolution
against nobility? Such is the myth. I look like a homeless
schiz and am often treated as such. And sure, I see and hear
what others can't. I call these visions the truth. Money doesn't
matter for manners, then. As for me, I don't know when

I'll take the pills again. No mighty flapping fish looking
to mate, I'm trying to not get kicked out of this conference,
sticking to myself. In New York, American power surges
through streets, making the ground hum. Here, too, I feel
everything at scale: at a distance from the collector node,
but same flows. How the hair on my arms salutes to electricity.
These drawls don't deceive; this is still empire. And oh,
forgive the dead wood of dry verse, as all empires consist,
mine included, of room corners, deigning to spawn and die.
Should the body feel alone? I suppose I'm crazy because I don't
feel at home in this body. No horizon here. Too many buildings,
silvery colours touched by less sky. For some reason I can't stop
remembering a muffler backfiring twice outside Joplin's regional
airport. Resistance ending as a barking cough through diseased
chrome, flakes of ferrous oxide shaking off, making the machine
porous—the extinguishing empire, in terminal decline. Now
the terminus: the broken exhaust pipe recreates home, to which
I admit myself. Here I am, empire, in your third-rate lecture halls,
mourning my upgrade from fourth-rate, finding no better welcome
and being unsurprised. Visual teaching strategies. Creation
of certificate programs. Narrative as the saviour balm. But
the empire, when it was grand! Like Lowell, it too was for me
something of a girl, in summer. But has been such a long, long time.

—from *The Malahat Review*

Kevin Irie

HOW TO PACK FOR INTERNMENT (150 POUNDS)

In 1942, the Government of Canada allowed Japanese Canadian adults to bring 150 pounds of luggage when they were taken by train to live in internment camps for the next three years.

Ask an elder. Ask someone old.
Learn to fold

clothes you can wear for more
than one season, for

more than one life. Same for shoes,
shirts. Whatever you choose

must last for a week, months, years
perhaps. It appears

even hope must
fit in a suitcase. Don't trust

where you're taken, where
you'll be sent. Enemy Alien, don't dare

ask. Take 150 pounds
in total. And, yes, it sounds

heavy, the weight of one person divided
by law. Just keep children provided

with toys, games, a gentle lie
so they won't see panic packed in your eye

when they look up and ask
where are we going? It's your task

to wrap truth like a *kimono* around them. Make
it look artful, careful to take

the best measure and length
of the future. It's the strength

of the passengers who smiled and waved
that impresses most, saved

by their grace, if not their skin,
their ticket in

to the train track
for boarding. Only the trains came back.

—from *The New Quarterly*

Vivek Sharma

IMAGINARY BREAKFAST WITH REAL PEOPLE

"There's nothing for us . . .
in this country," my Iraqi roommate says
the second morning after my arrival in Kelowna
as he breaks the bread into smaller chunks
and dunks it in cold milk. "Except for
the daily drudgery at $15.65."
He hands me a bowl of grapes and says:
"Aren't there good schools in India?"
I nod; he nods. We agree on things we don't
fully comprehend. Running his hand over
his thick beard, he proclaims like a prophet—
"We are here to clean white people's shit!
Do you know how to clean?" I shrug, my mind
oscillating in thick fogs of longing & separation,
propelled by a desire to escape or surrender. "I know
a place where they will hire you, but you will
have to make piss and shit your best friend. They even
pay two dollars extra." He forces a smile. In the kitchen,
a clogged sink is slowly suffocating in a sludge
of leftovers, and I dream of Tamor
heaving & gushing from the foothills
of Kanchenjunga, carrying no guilt
of shifting places. The heaviness percolates
in *drip, drip, drip* of decay. "If I were you," he says,
staring dreamily into space, "I'd finish school

and go back to India. There's nothing for us …"
His beard points eastward, to an imaginary home-
land he gave up on years ago in hopes of escaping
the *despairing and diabolic* ring that echoes
from the shallow waters of Karbala and ends
in the dregs of Tim Hortons coffee cups.

—from *The Fiddlehead*

Nofel

IN ARABIC

After Montréal, my beloved city

"My love lasts more than my lifetime," I say in Arabic.
Montréal & I shake our hips night & day in Arabic.

"We all live seven lives. There'll always be birds flocking in
even numbers," I heard on the subway in Arabic.

Over the seabed, fish snivelled when the son left. His eyes,
arrows tearing the moon. We sing, we pray in Arabic.

Arabic would've never been were it not for our eyes.
O yesteryear poising on eyelids, grey in Arabic.

If you're in love, why deny it? All endearments are one.
Paint me a mural in an alleyway in Arabic.

I watched his mouth trail my body, called him "ya habibi."
I sniffed his body hair. I let him lay in Arabic.

I cry & laugh better in English, my now mother tongue.
I have never found a mother per se in Arabic.

I dream of the word « revenir » & the rest is English
until I rise to the Moors' songs. We stay in Arabic.

Here, take this cradled tongue, this propagated love, this sown
hope. This isn't ghazal. It's your first bouquet in Arabic.

—from *Geist*

Sylvia Legris

IN THE WAKE OF

The deep lung recesses,
rumors of bees on speedwell,
no oxidative stress just
effortless pollination.

Dry-gust winds.
Dust winds its way
through discreet cracks.

Alveoli seized by misstep
of past future
forecast covariates.

Surface tension tweaks
to parts per million particulates.

—from *Granta*

Glenn Hayes

IT IS NOT HEART TO ESSAY

Your life changed in a knee-slap—
the kind you'd deliver at some corny joke—
when a tiny buzzing chorus
of brain cells just behind
your left eye, suddenly
blood-starved, died,

scrambling your head to babble.
Reading, writing, speaking wrecked,

leaving you trapped behind antique glass,
wondering why the world—which seems
lucid to you—peers back through bubbles,
waves, inclusions—befuddled.

Strangely, you can express yourself
most clearly through singing—
The *Yankee Doodle* grocery list,
the *Frère Jacques* meds you need,
the *Kumbaya* queries about your nieces.

But even though you'd been
a choir leader for a good part of your life,
you file the singing method
under N for Nuts.
What would your church friends think?

In an email you write,
"I do try to be papey—and happy—
buy it is not heart to essay."

Here Wordsworth
places his hands gently on your shoulders
like a doctor delivering the good news first,

O joy! that in our embers
Is something that doth live.

Some consolation for those ordained
to translate the music of the spheres
into dazzling flubs and clinkers.

—from *The Malahat Review*

Danielle Devereaux

LENDING LIBRARY, HEAVEN

Heaven's library held copies of every book that made a ding
'til the tech-wings got wind of e-readers—*My God,*
think of the space we'll save!—modern thinking isn't
really His thing, but real estate was at a premium.

Some rare first editions were dropped back to earth,
appearing in attics and Sally Anns, fun for the auctioneers
and *Antiques Roadshow* fans; the bulk tucked in storage.
Recall notices were sent to all library patrons, which

went well (they'd grown used to letting go), until Hitchcock
sent back *Silent Spring* with pages missing. Horrified,
the head archivist called Jesus Christ, going on and on—
the value of the printed page, respect for public property.
The dead, she wailed, *should know better by now, than the bloody*

living! Back at the office, Jesus finds the flask in his file cabinet.
Listen, Hitch, the librarians are pitching a fit. What in Pa's name
were you thinking? Stroking the hat in his lap, Hitchcock slowly
shakes his head. *It's that first chapter. The one where no birds*
sing. Christ, I just can't get enough of it.

—from *Geist*

Ozuyr Suloojee

THE LITTLE THINGS

Zurich is cold in January. The raclette and coffee at the airport were expensive, but the city was pretty, an obsidian lake and a broken sapphire sky; a sun with no warmth but lots of light. Our Airbnb host met us exactly on time, coming out of the apartment to let us in the gate, ignoring our earlier door knocks. We were on the way to Rome, via Milan, Tirano and the Bernina Express across the Alps, then to Istanbul, for a term of teaching abroad. We wandered the cobblestone city for a while. We bought chocolates and little Swiss-army knives—one for each of the four of us. The girls have them to this day. Mine was confiscated—it was part of my key ring—at a security check for a hockey game years later. The blade was little and dull, about an inch long, hardly sharp enough to prick a finger, let alone make a meaningful, or purposeful cut.

The apartment was strange and sweet and small. A ground floor—I think?—on a quiet street, not far from the lake. A short walk to the train station. Two rooms, low ceilings. Cat-print cushions. Old Hollywood posters; the poetics of bricolage. Straight in, a bathroom to the right, immediately off the little lobby, with an old chair and tiny artefacts on old desks, magnets on the fridge, frames on the wall. Audrey Hepburn + Cat, embroidered in bold colours on a pillow. Two bedrooms, pinwheeling off a main room—a combination of kitchen, living room and dining room. Everything just curated enough to be a modest ad in a local city magazine. In the dining room—in the very middle of everything—a table.

The girls—little, tired, but with new energy to take this new thing and place in—scattered. Backpacks dropped, shoes off, jackets and mitts and hats on the floor. A new, little soundtrack from all corners of the apartment now: "ewwww," "so cute" "Is that a butterfly collection?" "It smells funny" "I want that bed." "Can I put my lego there?" And so on. وهكذا، وهكذا. The table in the middle of the room was artfully piled with little things. Kitchen things, eating things. Dried flowers. Some books. Art. Travel. Zurich. Switzerland things. It had a metal top, sloped from each side to a drain near the bottom. A small, narrow channel, all around. A solid base. A medical examiner's table, an autopsy table, a coroner's table. I stared. Jen stared.

We didn't tell the girls of course. One would have been immensely and immediately fascinated at the macabre nature of this thing in the middle of our room, and that we were now eating our cereal at. The other would have paled, declared immediately that we (A), leave; (B) remove the table from any possible perspective where she might see it, or (C), cover it with a large enough blanket (impossible—it was huge), where she would give it side-eye and walk around the edges of the room not looking at it for three days. It stayed, and so did we, doing little things in little Zurich, waiting for our train to Chur, and then across the mountains. We stayed, eating meals out of our little coroner's table.

Today, maybe? I don't know anymore. In Gaza, Dr. Hani Bseiso, at a kitchen table, in a room with little things, in a house with cushions and curtains, and an armchair, and cold bright light streaming in from windows, and surrounded by tanks and Israeli soldiers, amputated the leg of his 16-year-old niece, Ahed. He used a saw, and a needle and thread.

I downloaded a video of this scene—after the amputation, because it felt important to have, to watch. In it, a young girl lies on a table, she blinks and turns to the camera. A hand reaches down to brush her cheek. A tear, maybe? Her right leg bandaged by the knee. Six men—I think?—attend to her. The camera pans left. A bottle on the table, a blue bag. A young man with an Adidas hoodie brushes her face, looks down and smiles at her.

This was the first thing I saw today in the social media litany. Wake up. Stay in bed. Check the feed. Sit up. Check the feed. Make some coffee. Check the Feed. Check. Check. Check. Like. Like. Share. Share. Like. Break apart.

It's the little things now, today, then, tomorrow, that I cannot look at anymore. I look at the kitchen table I built, that we had dinner at. That the cat jumps on. Piled with books, a few letters. A bank statement. A bottle of vitamins. A rock my nephew painted with "I Love you" on it. My little daughter, a year older than Ahed, sits at it, in a black BTS hoodie, eating a cupcake. It's cold outside, in Ottawa, in January.

I look at the little cardboard box on it, full of my not-so-little daughter's crochet supplies. A kufi she was hoping to make for her uncle (it's too small); spools of yarn from her grandmother's secret stash. Needles. Thread. A sharp pair of scissors.

I condemn chocolates and Swiss Army knives. I condemn raclette and expensive coffee. I condemn key-rings and cat cushions, and desks, and Audrey Hepburn. I condemn butterflies, and butterfly collections. And I condemn pillows and dried flowers. Trains, too. I condemn cobblestone streets. I condemn blunt saws and sharp scalpels, and purposeful cuts. I condemn houses, and rooms, and cameras, and bags, and bottles and hoodies. I condemn yarn and needles, and rocks that say I love you. I condemn language. All those little things.

—from *Janus Unbound*

George Moore

LOCAL FISHERMEN

The men must be doing something
always something hand over hand

coiling the rope preparing the skiff
going out ahead of the crowd

to find their best spot along the yellow coast
to collect rockweed in a pile so deep

the boat sinks to its rim at waterline
with biomass the cutting rake pulls in

or off in another direction of intertidal zone
knowing one place no one else goes

men must be doing in order to live
but doing becomes the living going out

beyond the last time beyond others
in a solitary direction but not alone

the wind does not bother you it is a friend
speaks in a thousand tongues greets you

coming in and going out but always
doing more it never sleeps takes no rest

the wind and the water and these men
must be doing something always going

—from *Queen's Quarterly*

Michael Ondaatje

LOCK

Reading the lines he loves
he slips them into a pocket,
wishes to die with his clothes
full of torn-free stanzas
and the telephone numbers
of his children in far cities

As if these were
all we need and want,
not the dog
or the silver bowl
not the brag of career
or ownership

Unless they can be used
—a bowl to beg with,
a howl to scent a friend,
a those torn lines remind us
how to recall

until we reach that horizon
and drop, or rise
like a canoe within a lock
to search the other half of the river,

where you might see your friends
as altered by this altitude as you
The fresh summer grass,
the smell of the view—
dark water, August paint

How I loved that lock when a saw it
all those summers ago,
when we arrived
out of a storm into its evening light,

and gave a stranger some wine
in a tin cup

Even then I wanted
to slip into the wet dark
rectangle and swim on
barefoot to other depths
where nothing could be seen
that was a further story

—from *The Walrus*

M. W. Miller

LOOKING FOR SOMETHING WRITTEN, THE IDEAL READER

In the early days we tried to turn away when he appeared in the alleys of the neighbourhood rummaging through the garbage cans and heaps

of trash, looking, he mumbled, for something written on scraps

of paper, or on anything at all, for something written, which he grumbling

claimed to never find, though he did find writing, as anybody could see, he had one rolling

eye, one eye never moved, he was gaunt, he was tall, and beneath his eyes, rolling

or not, were dark spaces, he wore an old torn filthy checkered suit, prison issue

it must have been, and his hair stood out in tufts, nobody in the neighbourhood could much stand his mumbling, his rummaging

or his stench, and especially objected to this idea of something written that only he understood or could judge, though he offered no standard, no aim, no helpful

critique of what fell short, of what only appeared to be written but was not, what kind of judge

could this be in a filthy prison-issue suit, one eye rolling, one eye dead, who untangled from empty tins and kitchen waste scraps

of paper on which something was certainly written but about which he mumbled there was not, letting each

piece drop to the pavement, fluttering, and shuffling

on to the next can or bin or pile, yet such was the strange attraction of his reeking passage through the alleys that in the end we felt

compelled to help, and so brought him torn pages of menus, old newspapers, novels, scripts, dissertations, ad copy, labels, signs, guides, maps and books

of instruction, and said that here was something

written, but with each example he only stumbled back as if startled, shook his head and mumbled, nothing written, and went on

with his meandering or unravelling route down the alleys, he
was lunatic

filthy and old, but still as cook, as crossing guard, as garbage
collector, as dishwasher, as news vendor, as server, we
gathered

along his route like exemplary characters in a children's
story set in a child's idea of a city, as if the buildings were
made of balloons and wooden blocks, curious, innocent, we
fell in

beside him and asked if he was looking for something written
in some way darker or more obscure, in the ink of drawn
blood, or etched by fire on stone, or invisibly

on the currents of air or water, or shaped into certainties of
ancient scripture, Chinese classic or Hebrew law, but he only
mumbled something

written and shambled off, which intrigued us, distracted us,
confused us, frustrated us, finally drove us to be mean, so
that we left

written taunts, curses and insults on scraps of paper slipped
into the garbage, or scattered along the alley as if in lentil
trails but leading nowhere, or rolled

into tubes and pushed through the meshes of torn fences or
broken shopping carts, it was strange how long

we went on like that, generations passing, however unwritten, as cooks, as crossing guards, as garbage collectors, as dishwashers, as news vendors, as servers we rose and fell

like the corn while our insults, curses and taunts never answered in time weakened, faltered, fell to more oblique warnings, then to counsels or advice, then to pleadings

requests and disclosures, then to confessions, intimacies and diary entries and finally to thoughts

we had just thought that day, through all of this

he was every day sighted less often, his once insistent stench receding, evaporating altogether even as we found that our discarded

written scraps, which every day with less reason we seeded along the alleys, were the next day gone, as if taken up in the night, by others

like him we imagined, with one eye rolling, reeking and in rags, we imagined, but it was impossible to know

what these others otherwise would be like, what they would be thinking or saying as they turned the scraps over in their hands.

—from *subTerrain*

Puneet Dutt

LUCKY

—It seemed every girl in school
had gotten knocked up;
—and every year it was the same jive—
Mom was 19 when she first met dad, and thought a kiss
would cuff her—night fever, night fever, she sang.
—Fast forward and my sister says, *Anyway, it's hot girl summer.*
At least now, you gonna be doin' you, girl.
During our walk in Rouge Woods
we find a robin's egg,
the fibrous yolk still clinging to the thin blue shell.
—How do you mourn a thing that—
even before the call—you know.
Like time-worn slot machines with their
handles sawed off—
Can you still get lucky?

—from *The Fiddlehead*

Sue Goyette

FROM *MONOCULTURE: A COMMENTARY OF MONOLOGUES*

(from the comment page of the potentially last—
and imagined—standing forest in Nova Scotia)

Leave reality at the door, or the opening or whatever bc this is one
wild departure from it all.

I definitely feel like I'm standing on a log between grief
and remembrance but I could go either way.

We were born naked, baby.

Ack! The pines are so punk!!!! There was one that looked
so much like Patti Smith I didn't want to leave. So that was cool. Her spirit
is so keen, you know? And that slouch of hers! Definitely pine-ish.

It's crazy that we buy a tree, decorate it, I mean adorn it with some pretty
gaudy shit, water it with the same mix we feed hummingbirds
and then just toss it out when we're done. Who do we think we are?

That first track of Parsifal. Or something by Missy. It's all about
the soundtrack.

Stay classy big rocks. We need you!

Who vapes in a forest?

What's most impressive is that it's all been made from dirt. Wild, eh?

What a triumph this forest has made of my afternoon. Thank you. Thank you.
Thank you.

The custodians probably aren't getting paid enough to keep it this pristine.
The hard work of veneering corruption, eh?

I watched a kid overwater all our bean plants in grade five. To kill them.
And I didn't say a thing. One girl, the one with the smelly markers, actually cried.
But he was the cool one. The one everyone wanted to hang out with.
That's it in a nutshell as far as I can tell.

I mean, if it's a comedy, it would be way funnier if we actually got to see the falling happening. Past tense is mostly for drama or memoir, but that's just me.

There is nothing normal about this. And I want this to go on the record. There. Is. Nothing. Normal. About. This.

What did Brecht say? A theatre without beer is just a museum?

Things definitely took a wondrous turn at the fallen cherry tree. We ate
what we could reach and only remembered to grieve the tree after. Yikes!
Hope that is allowed and doesn't ruin your exhibit. Circle of life, right?

He said saplings are the founding mothers of the rage that will corrode corporations from the bottom up. And that rage is as inevitable as revolution when you're surrounded by security. I made him add the word tree before revolution. So yeah, definitely a political experience.

I watched this clip of Céline Dion singing "All by Myself" shortly after her husband died. When she got to that note that unbuckles its safety line to soar into danger, her voice broke. The guy talking said it was because she got too emotional and emotionality can invade the integrity of the note held. Now I'm thinking: thank you Céline because that is what this visit to the forest has been like. My voice breaking at every damn tree.

I don't know. It felt like something was missing. A house or two. A cobbled path, a child actor pretending to be lost. To give this whole thing scale. Otherwise there's no way to measure its grandness, is there?

I wondered at the lack of struggle. How true can it be without struggle?

Will these be confidential? Because I have two things I want to say.

They didn't even flinch at the snow. So nonchalant and majestic, even when it flurried.

There was no place to actually stop. All the resting we did was just a break from the moving forward.

Hey Karen, thanks for the fountain of bug spray.

I did get a little freaked when they all became alert. Even the birds were turned off. Wait a minute, I thought, get me out of here, and it hit me: I had no idea which way was out. It was all up and down at this point.

Well it makes sense of the "lichen-hearted" she threw at me the other night.

It's not exactly what I'd call rural because there is this weird organic disco to it, like pizzazz-y if that makes sense. Some of those smaller plants are so unexpected and complex. So definitely not rural but not urban either. It's a species of place I don't think we have a name for. My girlfriend kept saying

it was like church which is close but there's something wilder,
like pre-pew, pre-ceiling. Wild architecture? See what I mean? The word
is on the tip of my tongue!! Anyone out there know what it is??

^Um, forest?

Swipe to the left: parking; swipe to the right: who the fuck knows?

Are these all the rebel trees? Or the toughest?

Any corporate foresters? Raise your hands so we can see you.

—from *Riddle Fence*

Ariel Gordon

A MUDLARKER'S DIARY

July 5, 2023: River level 6.60 feet

Lovely & cool out, we descend
to the waterline through upper banks

stuffed with willow & burdock sewn
together with the orange vines

of bindweed but topped with its innocent
white flowers. My phone intones: morning glory's

"invasive evil twin." I spot a med bottle
& an opalescent-edged milk glass jar buried

in the mud & somehow know both are
whole at first glance. What doesn't go in my bag?

Teal star-shaped plastic sunglasses. A navy
tampon applicator. A cerulean plastic flosser.

I do pick up snagged fishing lures & line,
mostly to get it out of my system.

I am rewarded when I spot a little ceramic crane
in half an inch of water & a broken plate

with a hand-painted bridge on it. A fistful of buttons
& a sherd with a geisha sitting in the grass

under trailing wisteria. No geese today,
but a mallard & six ducklings hug

the shoreline, moving on as I move along. One duckling
keeps skittering out into the middle

of the river, chirping at the sibs staying close
to the comforting drab of their mother.

Can I confirm that my right boot,
of my new brown rubber boots, has already

sprung a leak? My toes wet & wetter
as my eyes skip balefully from dead carp

to dead rodent to kitchen knife stuck
upright in the mud. We walk out though an abandoned

encampment & go for ice cream.
I get LaLa Lemon—which "fuses creaminess, sweetness

& lemon flavours"—in a waffle cone.
My toes, poached in riverwater, look like worms.

July 14, 2023: River level 6.52 feet

Shed rose petals & condoms
at the waterline. Wind-blown. Sewage-seeped.
Rip-rap revealed along the first stretch,

like a row of wonky appliances
at a denturist. Several sets
of old dock pilings, but no waterfowl.

At my feet, three/four dead crayfish,
exoskeletons gone white, bleached
by the sun. The water clearer

than usual: zebra mussels?
I wade & stoop, like a proper shorebird.
I spot a red faceted teardrop, paste ruby.

I find a blue bead, then a blue button.
My right boot is being infiltrated
again, the brown rubber the same

colour as the sandy river, the melted
slag. I startle an unseen bird
in the bush, possibly two. What is that worth?

Butterflies everywhere. Something orange falters,
lands on sand, flitters away. And black & white
winged grasshoppers, butterfly

mimics, flinging themselves
into the air. A big screwtop med, buried
head-first in the mud. Knowing

it was whole when I spotted it,
my eyes in. It will be the biggest med
on my shelf at home, where I rest my eyes.

The loose suck of mud & sand
as I tug the bot out! I have the river
to myself, though there are noises

from the big encampments up the bank,
the trees a curtain on a rod,
giving each of us the illusion

of privacy. I miss the amble
of adolescent geese. I haven't been slapped
by a beaver in ages.

May 10, 2024: River level 7.52 feet

Waterline survey

white plastic horse with short legs & pink mane
teal plastic seahorse
green/blue plastic medical waste
white plastic toothbrush with rounded base
cobalt blue plastic tampon applicator

white plastic cigarillo holder
yellow plastic/foam earplug
clear plastic medical waste
pink plastic medical waste
green plastic medical waste
white plastic cigarillo holder
clear plastic syrup bottle (Aunt Jemima)
red plastic medical waste
blue plastic flosser
white styrofoam chunk
blue plastic Nivea lip gloss tube
clear plastic disposable spoon
red plastic lid
red BIC lighter
white Styrofoam plate chunk
orange BIC lighter
orange plastic ball
pink plastic make-up tube
blue plastic medical waste
black plastic childproof medicine lid
white plastic cigarillo holder
white plastic Northern Lites Bait Co. Ltd. frozen minnows lid (salted)
white styrofoam lid for square container (also bait)
black plastic food container: microwave only
white/clear plastic IKEA packaging
clear plastic bubble tea straw
red plastic drink lid
fuchsia plastic tampon applicator
white/pink plastic COVID-19 rapid antigen test

clear plastic drink lid
clear bubble wrap sheet
white/yellow marijuana tubes
white/clear Tim Hortons iced coffee cup
mint green Nerf gun ammunition
clear plastic mini liquor bottle with yellow metal lid
clear plastic medicine dispensing cup (30 ml max)
black plastic wheely cart wheel
white plastic Wiffle ball
red plastic sewing scissor handle
green plastic super bouncy ball
yellow/red plastic/foam ear plug
white plastic liquid yogurt bottle
clear/yellow/purple/green/white Slurpee cup (Brain Freeze)
clear plastic applesauce cup w/foil lid
clear plastic disposable water bottle w/white plastic cap
yellow plastic balloon (popped)
blue plastic lid
pink/blue plastic Nerf gun ammunition

—from *subTerrain*

Petra Chambers

MY ANSWER TO THE QUESTION "HOW ARE YOU?" AT THE GROCERY STORE

There's a prehistoric spiny fish inside
me that freezes when it senses danger.
I'm also part primeval reptile. I have
an inner proto-rodent with a desperate
nuzzling reflex, pink and helpless and
forever seeking milk-based products.
These are the characters I'm stuck
with and none of them have names.

Despite the evolutionary advantages of
these built-in threat detection systems,
I sometimes neglect to notice danger.
From time to time, I have allowed
imperilment to sit by my hearth and
even—on occasion—sleep in my bed.

I bring my spiny fish, my vigilant
reptile and my inner proto-rodent
home and make them soup (resentfully).
I read them books. I tuck them in. They
stay awake all night, watchful, roaming,
snacking. I disown them. I attempt to
drown them, but they are buoyant
creatures and refuse to die.

How are you?

—from *Contemporary Verse 2*

John O'Neill

THE NEWS

When we heard the news
Russia had invaded Ukraine
my wife ate the radio. She

ate the television, her iPad and iPhone
in short order.
She did not bloat, however
or become irregular
but, in fact
more streamlined,
glass-hard, stiff-furred
lynx-like in the transition.

We sold our city house and moved up north.
North of grief, we thought.
But didn't believe. However

she stalks about the woods and won't speak
in any language that can be written
and refuses to keep a fire

though she burns with the memory
of her father's homeland. We don't

sit around and discuss it, we can't
stomach the details
or any reference to Putin
or Medvedev or Gerasimov.
I am lonely
and have laundered and drawered
my tongue and heart
with her refusal to be civilized.

It is all lies she shouts
from nerve-end treetops
the rivers of her eyes carving out
new channels
but it is not really shouting
it is a sound I've come to recognize

like a coyote or wolverine
at a kill or killing
the most human sound she
sings to deny.

—from *Prairie Fire*

Jennifer Gossoo

NÔHKOM

Nôhkom has a blue trailer by the Nicola River.
It don't feel like a trailer inside.
Nôhkom smokes but don't open no windows.
I can't smell a cigarette without thinking of her.

Nôhkom has a garden.
She shows us grandkids how to pinch peapods off the stalk.
Nôhkom knows the coyotes over the fence.
She throws them bones from her marrow stew.

Nôhkom serves orange Tang from a can,
And Kool-Aid Jell-O on white porcelain.
Nôhkom has a box of jellybeans that never empties.
She collects my drawings like some folk collect stamps.

Nôhkom has a small brown face,
And eyes the colour of creekbed clay.
Nôhkom looks light as a straw doll that the wind could carry,
But I seen her chase a griz in her mocs, bangin' on a trash can lid.

That was some skookum bear, she tells us later.
He was after my saskatoons!
I don't think my nôhkom minds, really,
Those skookum bears eating her saskatoons.

Nôhkom seen lights in the sky, once.
She lost them in the dark over Candy Mountain.
Nôhkom never spoke of spirits or spacemen,
But she weren't the only woman in my family to see lights.

Nôhkom explains about the valley hoodoos:
Men and women turned to earth by the Creator.
My teacher tells it different: erosion and sediment rock.
I like how Nôhkom tells it better.

I reckon Nôhkom cried when Papa died,
But nobody'd let me see.
I sat in the hall and ate green Jell-O from a cup.
It didn't taste half as good as Nôhkom's.

Nôhkom had eight daughters.
One daughter became my mother.
One daughter became an angel.
Six others became my aunties, women who laugh and holler
    and cuss like Nôhkom.

My nôhkom loved hummingbirds.
My nôhkom read *Where the Wild Things Are* in five voices.
My nôhkom showed me a jig in her kitchen, wearing a
    kerchief when the chemo took her hair.
It ended with "gibraltar."

—from *FreeFall*

Erin Wilson

ODE TO JOY

If one can escape
the fate of the news,
escape reality
          to enter reality,
one might live one's life
in the most radiant splendour.

Sink, I love you.

Water, dish rack, refrigerator, drain,
measuring cups.

Oven, philosopher friend.

Clock, most enduring brother.

Matches and candles,
you are my kindling.

Prescription medication,
hot water bottle, jean jacket.

Belt of worn leather, dearest.

Moccasins, sacred texts
worn closest to my soul.

Spider plant,
I have spent years
hating you

and yet you have remained
stalwart by my side.

Chairs. Chairs.
And the wood that you are made of,
nothing is taken for granted,
not even the lowliest screw.

Cast iron frying pans,
I do not take you lightly.

Flannels, I give you my eyelashes.

Books. Books. Books
and the varying bits of torn paper
stuck, at points, to mark pauses
in the critical flow,
my fingerprints are all over you.
Your fingerprints
are all over me.
Our fingerprints merge
to become one another.

I am alive
because
my tea towels say so.

Singular sunflower,
now emaciated,
plucked years ago
from our paltry flower garden,

popped unceremoniously
into a soda bottle in the window,
you are the art of the world.

Scent of coffee granules,
for God's sake, *Maxwell House*,
you baptize these air molecules.

There are times in my life
when my mind is aswoon
like a dancer, splashing
this way and that (multi-coloured
hand-hooked kitchen rug, heart!),
anointing all that anoints me.

While I'm at it (this naming),
Bach, Buckley, Beethoven,
YouTube, your thoughtful algorithms
bring to me the deepest music.

And these fingernails, these metacarpals, these lips, these lips
in an O,
thank you, thank you, thank you.

—from *Queen's Quarterly*

Richard Greene

ON THE USE OF THE SEXTANT

They knew how to pull the sun to the horizon
or fix a lunar that might do for days
of dead reckoning when the sky closed up.

In their wooden boats of spirit, the saints
saw little of God. Mostly the weather
of their affections, hunger for a name,

a better meal, some generous mouth to kiss,
and none of it could be quelled. It was not
a desolation. I think the best

of hearts can trust only upon occasion,
as banks of fog give way to sun, moon, stars,
in the ocean of things as they obscurely are.

—from *The Walrus*

Kayla Czaga

PAINKILLER

I put his ashes on the dog beach
I put his ashes on my bookshelf
I paid a company to put his ashes
inside a glass paperweight
I put his ashes off a cliff in Ucluelet
I put his ashes in the soil of my Norfolk pine
I put his ashes on a windowsill
of the Medicine Hat Best Western
I put his ashes inside a dream I had
I put his ashes onto a dollar bill
I put his ashes onto a second dollar bill
I put a dollar bill filled with his ashes
into a slot machine in Las Vegas
I put his ashes in a pond of greedy carp
I put his ashes onto a plate so I could
transfer them into an empty Advil bottle
Daddict Dadvil I put my dad's ashes
into my mouth and swallowed

—from *Room*

Sue Sinclair

PFEILSTORCH

Pfeilstorch is German for "arrow stork" and names a stork that is injured by an arrow while wintering in Africa then returns to Europe with the arrow stuck in its body. Wikipedia reports that as of 2003, about twenty-five Pfeilstörche have been documented in Germany. The Pfeilstorch referred to in the poem is on display at the Rostock Zoological Museum.

The problem is the stork looks immortal—like you can stick
a spear through its neck and it will hardly notice.
It seems to make of death a non-event,
the stuffing and mounting just a way of asserting its difference
from ordinary animals. It looks like an argument for God,
every feather—every vane of every feather—immaculately arranged,
devoted to the project of flight.

O cyborg angel, I see the marvel of you! How deftly
you defy both terror and logic. The arrow's shaft looks like just another
of nature's aberrations, a second pair of legs sticking out
from neck and chest, peculiar but benign. But I know a few things:
I've read the old stories, which tell that immortality is got through hardship,
always. I know I can stare into your glass eye in a way most
animals won't tolerate. I know what pain looks like when it's gone.

—from *Riddle Fence*

Karen Solie

PRIME LOCATION

Many years ago we viewed it
above the shop called simply
Convenience, a luxury
the apartment opposed, its floors

already soft, ceiling convex,
falling into the arms of gravity
as do we all. Vacant now
it's on the bus route

and so I see it too often,
first tentative tags given way
to bubble and wildstyle climbing
the brickwork, a paste-up of Shiva,

destroyer of worlds,
and the inscription *Fuck Landlords.*
As radiation accelerates the evolution
of the feral dogs of Chernobyl,

greed and neglect have hastened
the building's transition
into a state beyond purpose.
The land beneath it has its ear,

it inhales the amnesia of spores,
light filters through
its soaped windows like light
through the soaped windows

of all the deconsecrated churches
awaiting resurrection as condos
with paradisical walk scores.
They are released for a time

into a common meadow. But Denise is right:
"The past can't tell it *is*
the past," and won't go gently.
When a mysterious and purifying fire

prepares *Convenience* for demolition,
one more trace of us will vanish
with it, one less excuse
for sentimental nonsense, in this life

one has to be hard. Honestly,
it can't happen fast enough.
And the owner will say it's for the best,
he couldn't give that place away.

—from *The Walrus*

A. F. Moritz

QUIBBLE WITH HEGEL

The oak is an acorn
and blesses its origin: this oak, standing alone,
giving bunches—centuries—of acorns that drop to sleep
beneath it and are lightly nibbled
by squirrels, or collected first, some polished
and strung on threads, by children.
The cap and the glans once separated,
the cap is a little hat
for a small fingertip, or, turned over,
a little coracle bound for mystic Ireland
across a sidewalk puddle. This craft
is getting nowhere. In it, the studious
gaze of the children kneeling by the water
is the holy monk.

—from *The Malahat Review*

Dave Hickey

REAL ESTATE SIGN

Your face dangles from a tavern
    shingle, something a medieval inn

might prop against a solid beam,
    as if to say: the ale's fair standing here,

the straw pallets are comfortable,
    too. But then the corrugated plastic

catches the sunlight, and you are nothing
    if not a few hundred burnt dots

waving back and forth, a flap to nowhere
    in the wind. I can place you

among the league of faces
    who hawk shelter across the city:

champion of the fixer-upper, bestower
    of the retirement bungalow,

righteous shepherd of the Airbnb,
    you walk Hansel and Gretel

by the hand and tell them
    the witch next door has a way

with kids, loves company. All this
    to collect couples like acreage, draw them out

as property lines that fall away
   at the edge of a failing

cliff, marvel at what's left
   of the view. The other morning

I woke to a sign in my neighbour's
   yard, and the next day

it was gone, rarest of night
   blooming annuals.

People called, stopped,
   wanting to know what kind of flower

it was. What would it go for?
   they asked, afraid it would sell

sight unseen. They wanted to come
   back and count its petals,

as though it were the only
   one left of its kind, perfectly

set in a fitting of grass,
   and soon to vanish before them.

—from *The Malahat Review*

David O'Meara

RECESS

Granite outcrops in the schoolyard.
When you turned, maple and blue cedar,
an unkempt incline, fence, forest, a blur

of highway beyond the access road. Puddles
oozed in a downpour, mud flats
of the micro imagination. You could dig

canal rivulets with a stick you found.
Someone found the picture of a woman
on a matchbook we passed around,

boys and girls, awed by a new word, *bodice.*
Beyond hopscotch chalked-out boxes,
gravel started, then a diamond

where rules were schooled on strikes
and fouls. Mostly you ran. You climbed
metal bars planted in packed sand. Dennis

fell, and screamed. He got three
stitches on his chin. We were never told
that math won't end, or, like dreams, each face

we knew would soften and vanish. Instead,
we flipped quarters at the wall, and whoever
landed theirs closest kept them all.

—from *The Walrus*

Paul Moorehead

REQUIREMENT GALORE

To my eye, a loose button
is only a choking hazard.

But it aches when anyone
calls a dandelion a weed.

If I cried hexagons
I would stack my griefs

orderly as a beehive.
Oh, if I could weep

into a Klein bottle
I'd never have to know

which is the up. I could
take any geometry

of being, any tessellation,
any fractal zippering, any

Fibonacci counting and
counting of sunflower swirls

if,
    and only if

—from *Horseshoe*

Steve McOrmond

THE SCIENCE OF SKIPPING STONES

When the sun flares, the atmosphere
gets heated; satellites feel the drag,

their orbits decay. When the North
Atlantic throws a fit, shiny new Volvos

and the container ship they sailed out on
plunge to the bottom of the sea.

No match for the ocean, which plays
for keeps. Fair or foul, its moods

engulf us. Sometimes a grey-haired tyrant
with an axe to grind; sometimes a teenager

sobbing into their pillow for they know
not what. If you must disturb it, cast a stone

and see it step lively across the surface,
do not face it head-on. At just the right angle,

with sufficient velocity and spin, a rock
makes a little wave as it hits the water.

When the lift is strong enough, it propels
the rock up into the air again and again.

Choose a flat, smooth piece of sandstone
that fits in the palm of your hand, hook

your index finger around its edge for spin,
balance its heft between thumb and middle digit,

set your feet firmly in the sand, bend your knees
and, with a low sidearm pitch, let it rip.

One of these evenings, you'll find the perfect
stone – it was there all along – and watch

amazed as it gains altitude and momentum
with each bounce, pinballing into the cosmos.

The sky darkens by gradations. Pixel by pixel,
the star chart blinks into being.

—from *EVENT*

Susan White

SOME LATE FOR THEM TO BE AT THE FISH

Nan murmurs, mind lost in memory.
Her wiry curls are flattened against the pillow,
quilts tucked around her chest, eyes
fixed on the wall where

a single bulb glows
from a stage door at twilight,
rooms silhouetted within a wooden frame.
She knows a late night meant

a heavy load, skiff riding low in the water,
men up to their calves in cod,
sun setting as they sliced
and gutted and skinned and salted.

Nan purses her lips, squints,
tongue searching against the roof of her mouth.
I wait for her tongue to click,
the suction of her tutting.

Nothing comes.

The silence turns sibilant.
Her lips press into a thin line—*pssp pssp pssp*—
the thrifted print of a white cat, its blue eyes
pulling her from the past.

I see her fingers twitch
against the artificial softness of a polyester kitten
resting on her belly, tucked into warmth
stitched by her own hand.

Yes, I say.
Some late for them to be at the fish.

—from *Riddle Fence*

Megan Morrison

SOME QUESTIONS

Is it too late to wash the plastic container filled with gross fluffy mould.
Should I just throw it out instead.
Should I just get new plastic containers.
Is it too late to prevent osteoporosis.
Is it too late to prevent at least one form of cancer.
I don't care so much about tooth decay, is it too late to start caring about that.
Is it too late to read Proust.
Is there someone who can clarify this about Proust.
Is it too late to have children.
You said just one child, remember.
You said *yes* to Proust, then *no* to children, did I get that right.
Is there a preferred version of you that I can access some other way.
Is it too late to ask someone else about having children.
Is it me or does everyone seem pretty busy lately.
Is it too late to never have written a book and then suddenly write a book
about magical bears and the sleepy sickness and probably also my childhood.
And by is it too late, I mean, *is it too embarrassing*.
Is it too late to write something and then ask someone to read it.
Not even ask them, just send it to them and make them fucking read it.
Is the worse version of me actually the better version of me.
Is this the preferred version of me.
Am I usually wrong about things.
Would it change things, knowing this.

Is it too late to demand my liberation,
from what, I'm not sure, I'll keep you posted.
And your liberation too, you who are also not super liberated.
Is it too late though, now that there is disgust.
Is it true what they say about disgust.
By which I mean salivating, I mean gagging.
I mean actual disgust.
Can I wash this, dry this.
Will it always have the smell.

—from *Grain*

Cassandra Myers

SQUEAL

i.

Always an isolation, a gate click. Even city kids can imagine
what comes next. The sound—familiar to a family in a
farmhouse. It sharpens the knife within me. An animal's worst
fate is the slaughterhouse, but what about the bathhouse? To be
penned by heat and nowhere to run from the steam of a body
groomed to mount. We call barnyard rape *husbandry*, a white
gowning after our own brutal ceremony. I didn't know life
could birth that shape. Jagged and wobbling. My friend says,
You must've never lived on a farm.

It's all edible except the squeal. It's all audible except the grey
flat tongue spelling out *no*.

ii.

A moan is the most misunderstood mammalian sonic. When a
body pulls a car wreck from me and names it pleasure and
when I pull a white-eyed carp from my lily and name it
cumming—I moan all the same. I can only listen to smut
because every filmed mating herds a twist and snap
through my cavities like a stampede of slack bone, hoof of my
own wincing. But a squeal, a squeal always sounds like a pigtail
pulled, pitch of yank and no release, a scream trying to outdo
itself in the glasswear it shatters.

iii.

I walk home under streetlight and boys with grins like a schoolyard challenge me to a footrace. To run alongside and not away from, so it can't be a hunt. A shriek of a yes in my own galloping bones. At the end of the street is a boy with arms out for the finish line like an electric fence post. I reach for his outstretched hand. Expect to hear a clap like a whip against a ham bone. But instead, a flesh-lasso around my ribs. Stole the sow right out of my lungs. It wasn't a hunt, but a herding. Never trust a sickle with legs. You'll know it when you see one. It will look almost exactly like you.

—from *The Malahat Review*

Henry Heavyshield

STORYTELLING FOR YOUNG WARRIORS

i am not listening to stories. i am filling my quiver.
i am fasting with a copy of *the bell jar* in my lap. i will become
    lighter, stronger.
when i receive a new blackfoot name it will be 'strikes-with-a-pen.'
i call out for my auntie. there are no fathers here.
read to me at night & tomorrow i will build your mother's lodge.
i live off blood soup & chapters from dickens.
my party & i will count coup on your nation's favourite poet.
at their readings, we take scalps. scalps are a metaphor for plagiarism.
my bibliography is a winter count.
we don't capture horses anymore. we raid bookshelves.
when the corral is full, we give them away.
meet me at the buttes. the dust & ink mixed together looks like blood.
blood is what makes this real. listen to *naahsa* (grandma):
'make everything a gift with words.'

—from *EVENT*

Carolina Corcoran

SURFACING, COPENHAGEN HARBOUR

Being part Danish/part fish cut
me from soul-status.

But it had always been my dearest wish
to stand on legs and walk and live and
breathe and die and go to Ostend

or wherever it is Danes go when they're dead.
(Perhaps Ultima Thule in Greenland?) Besides
I'd gotten wind that a particular prince liked
a girl with soul.

Getting a soul is big business especially
among us half-breeds. We queued for hours,
centaurs satyrs manticores minotaurs, and when

I finally got to the front of the line, included
in the deal was tale-bifurcation and a pair
of high heels; the price was my voice.

I took it and paid, tongue
wrested from mouth, cut off at the root
knife forking my fins and then forced into shoes.

Perambulation was like walking on blades. In
the scramble of pain I reflexed a howl that
fell to the quay slimy and mute. I couldn't quite

swallow what I had done, everything silky
with blood and with spit. So spoiler
alert: I die in the end, I end it myself when

it comes clear no prince worth his salt likes
anything fishy or partial, impure.

There are bloodlines to think of, and not ones
that are new, not the kind that run
from your crotch to your shoes.

—from *Prairie Fire*

Darrell Epp

THAT'S NOT A PIÑATA, THAT'S A HORNETS' NEST

there's a war on, i mean negotiations have
broken down between the natural world
and the tonka toy dump trucks. steel-belted
giant wheels ran over a butterfly and don't
ask me why i'm screaming—why aren't *you?*
a secret wish, slammed into the boards;
the leaves of the paper birch, sandwiched
between a dying neuron and a cruel future.
martin buys a new shovel, says there's a
civilization below the one below this one
where angels never get tangled in power
lines, and there's a talking book guiding
all the runaways home, and kites ascend
forever. so start digging! over here, there's a
squid that changes colour when it's dreaming,
labour unrest at the thunderbolt factory, and
whispered hints of weightlessness between
system updates. my first gold star equals
the unpopped popcorn at the bottom of the
bag, so says ebay and facebook marketplace.
isn't it wild, just guessing on multiple-choice
tests, watching the wolves until the sun is
gone and you can't even tell whose carcass
they're dividing? this town was made for me.

—from *The Nashwaak Review*

Patricia Young

THE THING WITH THE WINGS

The day the thing with the wings turned up on our doorstep, the faucet ran dark ale. We drank. We celebrated. We'd always wanted a pet, house-trained and compliant, a blank slate on which to write our lives. Now here it was, no questions asked. We didn't wonder where it came from or why it growled at children walking past the house on their way home from school. Rubbing its head eased our anxieties. Stroking its belly lowered our heart rates. Before bed we told it stories—the abominable snowman, friendly giant, magic dragon. At night it slept at the bottom of our bed, but after a few weeks it wandered off. Was it climbing trees? Raiding birds' nests? Digging for shrews? The morning it returned, purring and reeking of aromatic fungi, we knew we'd made a terrible mistake. Blood dripped from our jaws. We looked at each other and then at the thing with the wings. It blinked slowly, the scales on its back glistening like eucalyptus leaves after rain.

—from *The Dalhousie Review*

Nicholas Bradley

TO THE BORDER AGENT WHO CONFISCATED MY BOOK OF POETRY

May you find it as fresh as contraband fruits and vegetables;
As intoxicating as wine, beer, or spirits in excess of the limit
set by the state Alcoholic Beverage Control Board;
As mysterious as the photographic film you are not permitted
to examine;
As dirty as soil unaccompanied by an import permit, as plants
and plant products no matter how free of pests they appear
to be;
As graceful and sinuous as cats, which are subject to inspection
and may be denied entry if they exhibit evidence of infectious
disease;
As quietly dangerous as ceramic tableware, which is neither
prohibited nor restricted, but when made in foreign
countries may contain lead in the glaze, which may seep
into food and beverages;
As free of viral zoonotic infections as the bodies of civets that
have been sufficiently processed to render them non-
infectious, as in the use of two percent formaldehyde or
hypertonic salts;
As specific as regulations concerning the importation of ivory,
including (but also excluding) ivory from warthogs and
antique objects made from ivory;

As complex as the process of importing or exporting a car, as
described in a separate brochure, which may be obtained
by writing to the appropriate PO Box in Washington, DC;
And as unambiguous, here and there, as the prohibition on
merchandise from embargoed countries, as transparent as
an unwrapped gift item;
And yes, I recognize that even if poetry meets all federal
standards, it might still be subject to additional requirements,
depending on what countries it was written in;
Consider it an unsolicited gift of no value, exempt from duty
and unsuitable for military applications;
I have signed and dated the book to affirm that I have made
truthful declarations;
But if it is not to your taste, then sell it for seventy cents on the
dollar. It's a free country.

—from *Grain*

Khashayar "Kess" Mohammadi

UBER-EATS GHAZAL

For Ruhul Kurd

how much grief can a body hold? how much water? it was posted
    online somewhere
anonymity is key while the executioner's blade hides somewhere

"DON'T KNOCK ON DOOR. DON'T RING DOORBELL.
    BABY SLEEPING."
the uber delivery driver has to drop the food off somewhere.

short bursts of remembrances. another death in the family.
the bus filled with mourners stops to have a meal somewhere.

the screen finds disaster and then slowly builds outwards.
the blood on all of our shoes must be drained somewhere.

there's a hum of a revolution, people gather in groups.
until a loud voice draws an arbitrary line somewhere.

our ancestors expected too much from us. we've tired of living.
we sit in tradition, yet unable to stay in our *somewhere.*

an empty cabin pearls the barren horizon,
for the next seeker who expects to rest somewhere.

from a distant haze in the sky spits forth an apology,
I wish God could keep silent until we built a home somewhere.

—from *EVENT*

Craig Francis Power

WALKING MY THREE-YEAR-OLD TO NANNY'S PLACE, EASTER SUNDAY 2017

"Dank ooze, dank ooze, dank ooze, dank ooze."
It took every hungover step of Cashin Avenue,

from the corner on Empire where once I rented
a basement apartment from a disreputable landlord, and wanted

nothing other than to sleep the clock around
forever, to the lights on Blackmarsh Road: the ground

still heaped in banks of filthy snow and shit
thawing in this, what's supposed to be spring—my daughter's mitts

and matching boots hot pink, against my better judgement—
before I understood what the hell she meant

by that. Took the turn toward Blackshire Courts. Climbing up the slope
much steeper than I remembered. Past the gas station, the
    boarded-up shops,

the factory bakery, the empty lots overgrown
with weeds, where we could see this entire shithole town

laid out below us: the high school, the dockyards, the courthouse,
    the penitentiary,
the brewery, the cathedral, the mental hospital, and the cemetery.

She kept saying this prayer
right to the door

of Nanny's low-rent dump:
Thanking the ground for holding us up.

—from *The Malahat Review*

Nancy Huggett

WE'RE DOUBLING DOWN, SAYS DARREN WOODS

Not even fiddling,
but feeding the fire
branch by branch, tree
by ancient tree. Bristlecone,
panania, redwood, chestnut,
black ash, whitebark pine. All
wisdom gone, frack by fractured
frack that cracks the earth for
molten cash. No time to Birnam
north, no time to heal those Permian
wounds that weep and flare
into the air that bathes our breath
in ash. We've doubled down,
restocked the pile that feeds
the flames that drive the heat
that burns the world around us
while we sleep.

—from *Prairie Fire*

Susan Glickman

WHAT I LEARNED FROM LIVING ABROAD

Wherever you go, locals love their home best
and assume you are visiting because your country is inferior

or you couldn't find a husband there
or occasionally both. This leads to some awkward conversations

but switching topics from politics and sex to food
guarantees a happier exchange.

Admiring babies is non-controversial
but do not pat their round heads or squeeze their chubby toes

without permission. The same goes for dogs
though folks are generally less indignant

if you cannot refrain from embracing their pets.
Whenever you enter a place of worship

cover your head and shut your mouth.
Remember how few of us have encountered a deity

and respect the attempts of so many to commune with one
even in places that represent the acquisition of wealth

through the oppression of citizens or by means of imperial conquest.
Having lit a candle in memory of your own persecuted ancestors

return to the topic of food or, failing that,
sit at a café table and sketch your surroundings.

People are offended when you take a photo without their permission
but delighted when you draw them—

everyone wants to ascend, so when prayer fails,
art will serve.

—from *The New Quarterly*

Emily Kedar

YELLOW FELT STARS

In the oldest barrack in Terezin
I find the room

where my grandmother slept,
the walls now plastered

in yellow felt stars.
I find the nursery

where she pretended
to be a nurse

to not be shot
or shipped off east

to join her parents.
They'd sent a letter:

they were heading out
for a trip to the country,

a code to let her know
it was their turn to die.

I'm walking through
the long hallways,

each step echoes *I'm still here.*
In the guestbook

left out for tourists
I write her name;

make my way out
to the green fields

where Jews grew food
for Nazis, where my grandfather

hid a few leaves
of lettuce to bring back inside.

A fist closes
inside of me. My grandfather

housed his memory
in my flesh.

I steady myself
with hands on the earth:

the green burn
of nettles climbs up

my skin and I take in
her grassy scent.

This little pain
all my own.

—from *The Malahat Review*

Misha Solomon

YOO-HOO

Yoo-hoo, do you love me?

Do you love me, yoo-hoo, do you love me, do you love what I'm wearing?

Yoo-hoo, you in the tank top, you in the tank top with the lavender hair, you sitting on the same café patio reading the novel I finished reading yesterday, do you want to talk about the novel?

Do you want, yoo-hoo, do you want to hear what I thought about the novel? Yoo-hoo, if you look my way maybe I'll say "yoo-hoo, I just read that novel, and I thought it was transformative/underwhelming/derivative/groundbreaking."

Yoo-hoo, do you see me, do you see me over here? I wore this tomato-red shirt so you could see me, yoo-hoo, you with the well-dressed baby, you look like you know nice shirts, yoo-hoo, do you want to tell me you like my shirt?

Over there, you over there, yoo-hoo, do you want to ask me what I'm working on? I just bought this new notebook to write one poem per day but, yoo-hoo, I've only written the date and my name and now I'm staring thoughtfully past you, hoping you'll think I'm actually staring at you and you could say "yoo-hoo, why are you staring at me" and I'd say "how embarrassing, yoo-hoo, I'm actually staring past you, thoughtfully, thinking thoughts, by the way, do you have the time, I didn't bring my phone, I'm trying to be more present?"

Yoo-hoo, do you have the time? Yoo-hoo, do you want to know why I need the time? I don't look like someone who needs to yoo-hoo for the time, isn't that intriguing?

Yoo-hoo, do you want to know?

Yoo-hoo, do you want?

I want, yoo-hoo, I want so much, yoo-hoo, you with the sexy calves, do you want me? Yoo-hoo, you can't have me, but I want a little yoo-hoo, I'd love a little yoo-hoo.

—from *Riddle Fence*

CONTRIBUTORS' COMMENTARY AND BIOGRAPHIES

JOHN WALL BARGER was born on Staten Island, New York, and grew up in Halifax, Nova Scotia. He's the author of six books of poems and one book of essays. His next poetry collection, *Resurrection Pie*, is forthcoming with LSU Press in 2026. He's a contract editor with Frontenac House.

Of "Darwin Award Song," Barger writes, "I've been chipping away at this poem for fourteen years. It began in 2011 as a draft called 'Deathbed Scene,' with the not-so-promising opening, 'Let the phone ring, it's not for who you are now.' In 2014, that draft merged with another poem I'd been working on about the Darwin Awards: that tongue-in-cheek 'honour' given to people who die as the result of absurd or reckless behaviour. I don't love the cruelty of this idea—that these people improve the species by removing themselves from the gene pool—but some of the Darwin Awards narratives are fascinating and heartbreaking. The Darwin Awards treat people's deaths as a kind of joke, and stay on the surface of the stories they tell. But poems have the ability to burrow underneath jokes and clichés. Anastasia Tutik and Miguel Ramos haunted me, and through writing about them I was able (slowly) to imagine them as people with families, feelings, inner worlds."

RONNA BLOOM is a Toronto based poet and educator and the author of eight books of poetry. Her work has been broadcast on CBC, recorded by the Canadian National Institute for the Blind, and translated into Bangla and Chinese. *A Possible Trust: The Poetry of Ronna Bloom*, selected with an introduction by Phil Hall, was published by Wilfrid Laurier University Press in 2023. Her new book, *In a Riptide*, is being published by Brick Books in 2025.

Of "Checkpoint of the Mouth," Bloom writes, "For a long time, I could say nothing about the events in Israel and Gaza. Only the suffering penetrated and the feeling of being heartbroken, angry, veering into despair and afraid to speak. I felt fractured. Sometime in February 2024, the poem came through. Once I heard the title, the rest queued up to get out. Now, I'm conflicted about publishing it here because nothing I write about this can hold enough grief and complexity."

NICHOLAS BRADLEY lives in Victoria, British Columbia—near Sitchanalth, in lək̓ʷəŋən territory. He teaches at the University of Victoria and is the author of two books of poetry: *Rain Shadow* (University of Alberta Press, 2018) and *Before Combustion* (Gaspereau Press, 2023).

Of "To the Border Agent Who Confiscated My Book of Poetry," Bradley writes, "The last word on crossing borders is the witticism attributed to Oscar Wilde: 'I have nothing to declare except my genius.' But what about the rest of us? Once, when I travelled to the US with a box of books in the trunk, the burly men in uniforms and mirrored sunglasses got me thinking about *declarations* and *customs*—about what poets have to say and how they say it. About content and form, in other words, and the ceremonies by which they are married. I was also wondering about the difference between 'as American as apple pie' and 'as Canadian as possible under the circumstances'—about what we have in common and what separates us. And about assumptions too. I presume that customs officers aren't avid readers of poetry, but who knows? I'd be thrilled to see my book in any reader's hands, never mind how it got there."

PETRA CHAMBERS (she/her) lives in the traditional territory of the PE'ntlatc and K'ómoks Nation. She writes creative nonfiction, poetry, fiction, and hybrid forms. Since 2024, her work has been published by *PRISM international*, *The Fiddlehead*, *Prairie Fire*, CV2, and the *Literary Review of Canada*, among others. Her first poem was nominated for a 2025 Pushcart Prize.

Of "My answer to the question 'how are you?' at the grocery store," Chambers writes, "Acknowledging mental illness still feels risky. A bit of rueful humour makes it easier. This poem emerged out of the exhausting, alienating experience of living a dual life: trying to resemble an untroubled, functional person while secretly waging epic, mythic-level battles within myself. It's about being caught off guard in the strange intimacy of a grocery store, our collective pantry, where we all seek comfort and necessities. When someone asks, 'how are you?' in a setting like that, the veil grows thin. If words have meaning, it feels like an invitation to drop the façade, but we are all supposed to pretend to be tame and untormented. How and when do we talk about mental illness and addiction? Where do these attempts occur? Do we haunt these interfaces and are we haunted by them? This was one of the first poems I wrote, way back in 2023. Any element of craft is purely accidental. My mother was a poet. We had a difficult relationship. I am still learning to trust poetry. I pulled the spiny fish, primeval reptile, and proto-rodent from Polyvagal theory, with eternal gratitude to Stephen Porges for developing a framework that helps me feel less broken."

CAROLINA CORCORAN was born in Whitehorse, Yukon, on the traditional territory of the Ta'an Kwäch'än Council and the Kwanlin Dün First Nation. Her work has appeared in a number of journals, including *Arc Poetry Magazine*, *Crannóg*, and *Magma*.

Of "Surfacing, Copenhagen Harbour," Corcoran writes, "A bronze statue of the Little Mermaid was erected in Copenhagen Harbour in 1913. She sits slouched on a rock a few feet offshore, staring into the Nordic abyss. This poem is one of a whole whack of poems based on fairy tales. I like the bits Disney declined to depict."

KAYLA CZAGA lives in the Township of Esquimalt with her wife and two senior cats. She is the author of the poetry collections *For Your Safety Please Hold On* (Nightwood Editions, 2014), *Dunk Tank* (House of Anansi, 2019), and *Midway* (House of Anansi, 2024).

Of "Painkiller," Czaga writes, "My father did not want to be buried in a cemetery or cremated. Instead, he wanted his body dumped into the ocean. We weren't sure if it was legal to do that, so I convinced him to be cremated, and told him I'd take his ashes on trips with me and spread them around. Since 2017, I've been carrying around a small glass vial filled with my father's ashes. When I'm someplace new, I ask the ashes if they'd like to be placed there. Then I listen for an answer. It could be me just listening to me, but I try to honour whatever answer I hear. I've been surprised by the answers of the ashes. For example, the ashes did not want to be scattered in the Danube (though my father was born in Hungary), but they were interested in various spaces in Las Vegas. 'Painkiller' is an ongoing document, a collaboration with my father's ashes."

DANIELLE DEVEREAUX lives in St. John's, Newfoundland. Her first full-length poetry collection, *The Chrome Chair*, was published by Riddle Fence Debuts in spring 2024. Her chapbook, *Cardiogram*, is published by Baseline Press (2011). The chapbook's title poem appeared in *The Best Canadian Poetry in English 2011*.

Devereaux writes, "'Lending Library, Heaven' is part of a series of poems I've written in response to the life and work of Rachel Carson, the author of *Silent Spring*. Published in 1962, *Silent Spring* is often referred to as the catalyst of the modern environmental movement. The first chapter of the book describes a fictional American town, once lush with prosperous farmland, left barren and decrepit, devastated by the negative effects of pesticide use. It is also silent, as there are no birds left to sing. Hitchcock in this poem is of course Alfred Hitchcock, the famous director of many thriller/horror films, including *The Birds* (1963). Rachel Carson is interesting to me for all sorts of reasons, but one of the things I was thinking about when I was writing this series is the idea of fame and who gets to be an icon, so sometimes other famous people show up in the poems. Carson died just two years after *Silent Spring* was published. She was fifty-six. Though she knew it was having an impact, she couldn't have foreseen the way her book would come to influence the world. At one point I was trying to figure out how to write a PhD about Rachel Carson, but making up poems where she could still exist in a way (in heaven, in letters) was more fun."

IRINA DUMITRESCU was born in Bucharest, grew up in Toronto, and now teaches medieval literature at the University of Bonn, in Germany. She is the editor of *Rumba Under Fire: The Arts of Survival from West Point to Delhi* (Punctum Books, 2016), a collection of essays and poems about the sustaining role of arts and humanities in times of crisis.

Of "Criseyde," Dumitrescu writes, "The summer I wrote this poem I was teaching an MA seminar on Chaucer's long poem *Troilus and Criseyde*. Our building was hot and the air conditioning was not working, and we were translating the Middle English even more slowly than usual, or so it felt. I thought about Chaucer's attempt to understand Criseyde, this imagined woman who became a byword for betrayal in the European literary tradition—during the Trojan siege, she is forced to leave her lover, Troilus, but ultimately takes up with Diomede, a Greek warrior fighting on the other side. It struck me that, as the daughter of a seer, Criseyde must have known all along that her city would be destroyed, that everything she knew and loved would disappear. Even in her lightest moments, she could never escape the knowledge of that doom. Still in the muggy spell of translation, I left the classroom and immediately wrote down a few lines, short ones, to try and catch her while she was still close."

Born in New Delhi, India, and raised in Jersey City, New Jersey, PUNEET DUTT is a poet and editor based in Markham, Ontario. Her debut collection, *The Better Monsters* (Mansfield Press, 2017), was a Trillium Award finalist. A poetry editor at *The Fiddlehead*, she serves on the boards of *Canthius* and *The Ex-Puritan* and holds an MA in English from Toronto Metropolitan University.

Dutt writes, "'Lucky' was written in the early days of the pandemic, a time of deep uncertainty and grief. My sister was staying with us while mourning a personal loss, and my husband and I were trying for a child. With so much loss around us—in the news, in our home—I found myself holding on to the hope of new life. I kept thinking about how school programs warned us against teen pregnancy, how simple they made it seem compared to the complexity of trying now. I also remembered a story my mother once told me about my parents' first date—watching *Saturday Night Fever*—and how, as a teenager, she was so naive she believed a kiss could cause pregnancy. The poem came together when I found a broken robin's egg—so blue, so perfect—during a walk with my sister: an image of both beauty and loss. Later, while revising, I recalled visiting a Niagara Falls casino where the handles on old slot machines had been removed, yet people still tried to play them, hoping to get lucky. That image stayed with me. The poem became a meditation on longing, risk, and the quiet persistence of hope—even when we're unsure if things still work."

DARRELL EPP lives in Hamilton, Ontario, and is inspired by its beauty every day. He has published six books of poetry and hopes to publish many more.

Of "That's Not a Piñata, That's a Hornets' Nest," Epp writes, "I don't remember writing this poem. I do remember often thinking to myself, while writing poems, 'Wouldn't it be great to write something that thrilled a reader the way reading Gerard Manley Hopkins thrilled me ...' Not sure it's ever happened, but I promise to keep trying!"

SUSAN GLICKMAN grew up in Montreal and lives in Toronto, where she works as a freelance editor and is learning to paint. She is the author of eight books of poetry, four novels for adults, three novels for children, a work of literary history, and a selection of essays.

Glickman writes, "'What I Learned from Living Abroad' was inspired by the four years I spent in Europe as a young person. All poets are outsiders—if we weren't, we wouldn't scrutinize the world the way we do—but during that time I was particularly aware of this status not only as a Canadian, but more particularly as an Ashkenazi Jew in the diaspora. Most people were at home where they lived. I was not. This poem became part of my most recent collection, *Cathedral/Grove* (Signal Editions, 2023), in which several other pieces are written from the same uneasy perspective. It is written in couplets, most of which employ the device of enjambment: that is, they run over the stanza break instead of honouring the form. In the final two stanzas that tension resolves; at the same time, the poem concludes on a serious reflection rather than the more playful ones that have preceded it. The revelation of the last line only came to me while writing the poem about forty-five years after actually living abroad, but it still feels profoundly true!"

ARIEL GORDON is a Winnipeg/Treaty 1 territory-based writer, editor, and enthusiast. She is the ringleader of Writes of Spring, an NPM project with Plume Winnipeg that appears in the *Winnipeg Free Press*. Her most recent book of poetry is *Siteseeing: Writing nature & climate change across the prairies* (At Bay Press, 2023), written in collaboration with Brenda Schmidt and nominated for a Saskatchewan Book Award.

Of "A mudlarker's diary," Gordon writes, "I have been mudlarking since 2020 but I only started to write about those experiences—walking a silty river in the middle of the city, surrounded by bridges and train tracks and homeless encampments, filling my pockets with old glass and china—in the last few years. I have discovered that I am happiest when I am muddy, walking in a foot of river water, my eyes sorting bivalve shells from sherds of china, stones from wonky marbles. Was what I was finding treasure or just settler garbage? I still don't know, but I feel more connected to urban nature. I feel enmeshed."

JENNIFER GOSSOO is a writer from the Nicola Valley, British Columbia. Her poems and essays have appeared in *FreeFall Magazine*, *The Malahat Review*, *Geist*, and others. She holds a BFA in art history and creative writing from the University of Victoria.

Of "Nôhkom," Gossoo writes, "This poem is a reflective piece rooted in the practice of remembering. I use each stanza to paint a new set of memories for readers who didn't know my nôhkom (but may have known someone like her). My purpose in writing this memory-centric piece was threefold: 1) To share details of a lived human experience in rural, 90s-era British Columbia, 2) To retrospectively explore aspects of the ancestry I share with my grandmother, 3) To recount and record the scenes, habits, and moments which, in my mind, most accurately convey her essence to a reader."

SUE GOYETTE lives in K'jipuktuk (Halifax) and is a poet and educator. She's published ten books of poems and a novel. Her most recent collection is *Future Howl* (Gaspereau Press, 2025). Her work has been translated into French, Spanish, and German and has been featured in films, plays, musical compositions, subways, buses, spray painted on a sidewalk, and tattooed.

Of "from *Monoculture: A commentary of monologues*," Goyette writes, "My plan was to write poems about the deplorable clearcutting practices in Nova Scotia, but when I started writing *Monoculture* all I could come up with were inevitable versions of *dude, don't cut down old-growth, beautiful trees* with line and stanza breaks. The poetic dilemma was how to transform the obvious into something that could be surprising enough to potentially initiate conversations while recharging the way we think and care for our forests. I found myself sitting with this challenge for weeks until one morning I imagined the voice of someone visiting the last standing forest in Nova Scotia for the first time. Then I imagined another visitor and soon found myself writing short monologues/commentaries for that imagined forest's website. I cannot tell you how invigorating writing this was. Some comments made me laugh out loud. Some made me cry. I often wondered during the process if I could get away with having so much fun. What's been surprising is how meaningful the interactive readings of the collection have been out in the world and how many readers feel connected to their own specific tree and how, in this way, we become a forest of tree memories."

RICHARD GREENE, a Newfoundlander, teaches creative writing at the University of Toronto. He is the author of internationally acclaimed biographies of Edith Sitwell and Graham Greene, as well as four volumes of poetry with a fifth, *Cannibal Rats*, forthcoming from Véhicule Press in 2026. His poetry has been recognized by the National Magazine Awards (Gold) and Governor General's Literary Awards.

Of "On the Use of the Sextant," Greene writes, "I am fascinated by the sea, by weather, and by the coastline of Newfoundland, where I spend much of my time. This piece opens with an account of how a sextant measures angles. Metaphorically, the poem is about the gaps in what we know, and how we live by dead reckoning, that is, by a judgment of where we are and where we are headed when there is nothing to guide us. Old sailors would work their way through foul weather and closed skies, hoping to get a fix on the sun at noon or on other celestial bodies—and between those moments of certainty there was just desire, the exercise of a mariner's skill, and trust in some order that is glimpsed from time to time."

GLENN HAYES lives in Newmarket, Ontario. His work has appeared in many Canadian magazines, reviews, and journals, including *The Antigonish Review*, *Arc Poetry Magazine*, CV2, *The Dalhousie Review*, EVENT, *The Fiddlehead*, *FreeFall*, *Grain*, *The Malahat Review*, *The Nashwaak Review*, *The New Quarterly*, *Prairie Fire*, *Qwerty*, and *Vallum*. His poems have been shortlisted nine times for various poetry contests.

Of "It Is Not Heart to Essay," Hayes writes, "I wrote the first version of this poem in 2019. It is about my aunt's struggles with both speaking and writing after a stroke left her with aphasia.

The original inspiration (and the title) came from an email she wrote. Over the years, the poem saw many revisions. Images, words, stanzas were cut or added. I expanded the section on my aunt's love of music and her refusal to communicate through singing. A cluster of cells became a chorus of cells. Wordsworth stepped into the poem to place his hands on my aunt's shoulders and to console her with his poetry. The ending I was looking for opened the poem to include "those ordained / to translate the music of the spheres / into dazzling flubs and clinkers."

HENRY HEAVYSHIELD is a Blackfoot reader and writer from Kainai (Blood Tribe First Nation). He is a Writers' Trust Bronwen Wallace Award finalist (2024, short fiction category), was on the 2025 CBC Short Story Prize longlist, and is an Indigenous Voices Awards finalist for short fiction and poetry. His work has been featured in several literary journals and anthologies. He currently works as a communications officer for Blood Tribe Administration.

Of "Storytelling for Young Warriors," Heavyshield writes, "In the summer of 2024, I had landed on a working definition of poetry as 'the pursuit of joy through language.' I was inspired by fellow Indigenous poets and writers who celebrate NDN joy as a daily form of active resistance. This poem is my attempt to navigate the many definitions of Indigenous (specifically Blackfoot) masculinities using that framework. The poem started off as a kind of message I wanted to pass onto my nephews but blossomed into something more. Growing up, my cousins and I were faced with competing images of what it meant to be a 'warrior.' There were the settler-colonial stereotypes: savage, merciless, unintelligent. And on the other hand, we had the lessons we gleaned from stories we heard from our parents, aunts, and uncles: men and women who were courageous for their kindness, humility, generosity, and intellect. I was curious what would it look like for Blackfoot storytelling traditions to 'count coup' on writers (some favourites of mine) from the Western canon? Or, how could I explain my bookish or literary pursuits in terms that the Old People would understand? I guess this poem is my way of 'actin' up' in the face of those stereotypes."

DAVE HICKEY is the coordinator of the Applied Communication, Leadership, and Culture program at the University of Prince Edward Island. He is the author of two books of poetry, *In the Lights of a Midnight Plow* (Biblioasis, 2006) and *Open Air Bindery* (Biblioasis, 2011). He lives on the south shore of PEI, a stone's throw from Tea Hill Park, and not far from Oqo'sikji'j.

Of "Real Estate Sign," Hickey writes, "A friend of my neighbour's stuck a real estate sign in his lawn one night. It was supposed to be a practical joke, but even after he'd taken it down, people asked about the house, cruised by slowly to see if it sold. The humour was, like the housing market itself, hard to fathom, and not so much funny as cruel."

NANCY HUGGETT writes, lives, and caregives on the unceded Territory of the Anishinaabe Algonquin Nation (Ottawa, Canada). Her work has been published in *EVENT*, *The Ex-Puritan*, *One Art*, *Pinhole Poetry*, *Poetry Northwest*, *Prairie Fire*, and *SWWIM*. She's won some awards (including the 2024 RBC-PEN Canada Emerging Voices Award) and a gazillion rejections. She keeps writing.

Huggett writes, "October 11, 2023 *New York Times*: The acquisition of Pioneer Natural Resources, Exxon's largest since its merger with Mobil in 1999, is a bet that US energy policy will not move against fossil fuels in a major way. 'We're doubling down on our organizations and capabilities,' said Darren Woods, Exxon's chief executive. 'Doubling Down' is a rant that tumbled onto the page with its rhythm intact. I had just read environmental activist Bill McKibben's Substack post (which included the Darren Woods quote) about Exxon acquiring one of the largest fracking operators in the world and the poem emerged in a flash of anger at the audacity and stupidity of corporate greed and ignorance in our deepening reliance on fossil fuels. I did a bit more research to build a word bank that might help augment the rhythm. The only rabbit hole I went down—which gave me the line 'No time to Birnam north'—was learning about how trees shift their location as a long-term response to climate change. Obviously, these shifts take millennia, and we don't have that kind of time. I had this clear image of all these corporate moguls sitting around a fire, this fire of a planet, feeding the flames with these achingly beautiful and endangered trees, laughing and enjoying themselves as ecosystems disappear."

KEVIN IRIE is a Japanese Canadian born in Toronto. In 2024, he won *Grain*'s poetry contest, second prize in *Prairie Fire*'s poetry contest, and third prize in *The New Quarterly*'s poetry contest. He is in *The Gate of Memory: Poems by Descendants of Nikkei Wartime Incarceration* (Haymarket Books, 2025). His next book is *Evacuations* (University of Alberta Press, 2026).

Of "How to Pack for Internment (150 pounds)," Irie writes, "Both sides of my family were interned in British Columbia during World War Two. Forced to leave Vancouver, they were put on trains and only allowed to bring 150 pounds of luggage, not knowing where they were going or for how long. Some internees, who were children at the time, thought they were going on a big trip, a family holiday. Whether it is the depiction described in Joy Kogawa's poem 'What Do I Remember of the Evacuation' or what was recounted in family memories, adults were careful to shield the young, a task both heroic and heartbreaking."

EMILY KEDAR lives between Salt Spring Island, British Columbia, and Toronto, where she practices psychotherapy and writes poetry. Emily's work has appeared in *One Art*, *The Malahat Review*, *The Maynard*, *Bellevue Literary Review*, and *Poetry Pause*, among other publications. She received her MFA through Pacific University, where she delighted in being part of a rigorous and supportive community.

Of "Yellow Felt Stars," Emily writes, "One of my jobs as a poet has been to help turn ghosts into ancestors. This poem is a hard-won jewel from an emotionally confronting trip to Prague and the concentration camp where my grandparents were interned during the Holocaust. This poem needed to be written—not just for its own sake, or for my own understanding, but as a gift for my lineage's liberation. Poetry can be that kind of alchemy. I will never forget walking down the halls of Terezin, standing in the wide fields, feeling both the horror of what happened there and the absolute miracle that I was alive and had the courage to return. This poem speaks to the power of personal pilgrimage, of transforming grief into words."

CONOR KERR has written books.

Kerr writes, "Damn, rereading 'Fancy University Boy' and I'm struck by how autobio it is. I wrote this poem during a long, sad winter in Edmonton where I spent most nights at the pub thinking about all the life choices that had brought me to this place. It's included in the *Beaver Hills Forever* collection. It's essentially me trying to come to terms with my university undergrad experience, which I think was largely horrible. I spent most of it trying to get out. Ironic since I'm back in that same department now. I just remember feeling incredibly uncomfortable with how hillbilly Métis I was (am). And the constant embarrassment I felt and how I was drunk for most of it, coping mechanisms. I think 'Fancy University Boy' ends with a note to the future, or at least my future, the proposed one for what could happen. Spoiler for *Beaver Hills Forever*, that's not exactly what happens to Fancy University Boy."

EVELYN LAU is a lifelong Vancouverite who has published fifteen books, including ten volumes of poetry. Her poetry has received the Milton Acorn Award, the Pat Lowther Award, the Fred Cogswell Award, and a National Magazine Award. From 2011 to 2014, she served as Vancouver's Poet Laureate. Evelyn's most recent collection is *Parade of Storms* (Anvil, 2025).

Of "Cursing, Flailing," Lau writes, "Much to the chagrin of friends and fellow writers, I have always been enamoured with America, despite its flaws. My travel bucket list involved setting foot in every state; I've visited thirty, but that number isn't likely to grow in the coming years, given the current (heartbreaking, unforeseen) tension between our countries. 'Cursing, Flailing' was inspired by a post-COVID road trip in which I was thinking about some of the clichés and eccentricities of the US, during a time fraught with debate over the pandemic and climate change. Admittedly there would be few sights more upsetting to those who are zero-waste practitioners than the 'free breakfast' room at any American motel . . . but honestly, I would love to see the return of plastic straws!!"

Originally from Winnipeg, SYLVIA LEGRIS lives in Saskatoon. Her poetry collections include *The Principle of Rapid Peering* (Corsair/New Directions, 2024) and *Garden Physic* (Granta Books, 2022; New Directions, 2021).

Legris writes, "'In the Wake of' is from *Sleep Gate* (yet unpublished), a poetry collection that explores dream and sleep cycles. Many of these poems were written in the wake of COVID and in the wake of various extreme weather events, including wildfires both west and north of Saskatoon. How unreal it seemed that I'd shifted from wearing masks indoors at the height of COVID to wearing them outdoors because of the smoke."

STEVE MCORMOND lives in Toronto and has published four books of poetry. His most recent collection is *Reckon* (Brick Books, 2018). Originally from Prince Edward Island, he is a graduate of the creative writing program at the University of New Brunswick and a past recipient of the J. M. Abraham Atlantic Poetry Award and the P. K. Page Founders' Award for Poetry.

McOrmond writes, "'The Science of Skipping Stones' is inspired by an old photograph of the late PEI poet John Smith skipping a stone on the Island's north shore. Smith's poems, deeply informed by physics and mathematics, often imagine alternate universes in which the laws of nature as we know them do not apply. The world record for the number of skips, according to the *Guinness Book of Records*, is a gravity-defying 88, set by Kurt 'Mountain Man' Steiner in 2013. I don't remember how old I was when I learned to skip stones, or who taught me, which may explain why it feels like magic. The sky's the limit."

ESTLIN MCPHEE is a writer and librarian who grew up in a small town on the territories of the Kwantlen, Katzie, Matsqui, and Semiahmoo First Nations. For many years, Estlin co-organized REVERB, a queer reading series in Vancouver. They are the author of the poetry book *In Your Nature* (Brick Books, 2025) and the chapbook *Shapeshifters* (Rahila's Ghost Press, 2018).

Of "Gay Messiah," McPhee writes, "This poem began for me a very long time ago, with the image of someone at the piano, playing songs learned from the dead, and with the speaker of the poem singing along from a seated position on the carpet. Nothing else from the first—or second, third, or even fifth—draft remains in the final version of the poem, which borrows its title from a Rufus Wainwright song that appeared on his fourth studio album, *Want Two*, in 2004. I don't know how that original image morphed into an imaginary party of queer historical figures performing a magical ritual together, but at some point the fiction of these characters' interaction became a vehicle for exploring an emotional truth. Throughout my book *In Your Nature*, I use the idea and language of 'turning' frequently, to reflect on and play with its different meanings—transformation, movement, change, betrayal, beginning, ending. In this poem, 'turn' also indicates the speaker stepping into their power: the next move belongs to them."

M. W. MILLER is a British Columbia writer who has appeared in *The Malahat Review*, *The Capilano Review*, *The Dalhousie Review*, *The Antigonish Review*, *Unlikely Stories Mark V*, and of course *subTerrain*, among other publications.

Miller writes, "My Canadian homelands are the neighbourhood of Mount Pleasant in Vancouver, the slopes of New Westminster with the Fraser River nearby. 'Looking for Something Written, the Ideal Reader' takes place as if on numerous cloudy afternoons in Mount Pleasant."

KHASHAYAR "KESS" MOHAMMADI is an Iranian-born, Toronto-based poet and translator. Their most recent poetry collection, *Book of Interruptions*, is out with Wolsak & Wynn. Their translation of Ghazal Mosadeq's *Andarznama* is forthcoming from Ugly Duckling Presse.

Of "Uber-Eats Ghazal" Mohammadi writes, "I wrote this poem while under financial duress, and trying my best to make ends meet by using the Uber Eats app as a day job. On my lunch break one day, I stopped in Brampton (famous for its Indian diaspora) for chai and sweets. I wrote the poem for my Muslim elder Rahat Kurd, with whom I always discuss the issues of home and belonging."

GEORGE MOORE is originally from Colorado, where he taught at the University of Colorado, Boulder, before moving to Nova Scotia with his wife, the Canadian author Tammy Armstrong, in 2014. They live and write in the lobster fishing village of Shag Harbour, well-known for its UFO museum. His sixth collection, *Saint Agnes Outside the Walls* (FutureCycle), was published in 2016.

Of "Local Fishermen" Moore writes, "We live just off the government wharf in Shag Harbour and hear and watch the constant activity of lobstermen going out each morning before dawn and often returning late at night. The sounds of the boats seem to be a constant vibration, a low hum of diesel engines and lobstermen tossing down bait boxes, stacking traps, or unloading the day's haul. And, in this particular poem, the gathering of rockweed, raked into mountains on small skiffs and motored back to the wharf. Their livelihood becomes a rhythm of life as a process, full of the sea, of hard work, and of constant activity. That was a rhythm that seemed to write itself into the poetry."

PAUL MOOREHEAD is a writer in St. John's, Newfoundland and Labrador. His poetry has appeared in *Pinhole Poetry*, *Riddle Fence*, *Horseshoe Literary Magazine*, *Turnstyle: the SABR Journal of Baseball Arts*, the anthology *Brand New Season* (Orenaug Mountain Publishing, 2025), and in his first poetry collection, *Green* (Breakwater Books, 2025).

Moorehead writes, "'Requirement Galore' is a nonsense poem, but the nonsense is borrowed from the language of mathematics and geometry, a camouflage of organization that the poem's speaker uses in service of his melancholy. We live in a natural world of beautiful patterns, of beehives and sunflowers, and the poem attempts to use those patterns to weave a sense of wonder that the speaker cannot quite grasp. He sees only the constraints of those patterns, the 'requirement galore' of the title. He is perhaps willing to accept this ordering of the world, but nothing comes to him after the poem's concluding 'if / and only if': the speaker doesn't know what would be logically equivalent to a permission for his acceptance of wonder. I feel a bit sorry for the speaker, who is obviously a bit of a drag. He is not (exactly) me."

A. F. MORITZ lives in Toronto. His 2024 book, *Great Silent Ballad* (Anansi), which includes "Quibble with Hegel," received the 2025 Al and Eurithe Purdy Poetry Prize. *As Far As You Know*

(Anansi, 2020) was a finalist for the Trillium Award. With poet and fiction writer Theresa Moritz, he has co-written biographies of Stephen Leacock and Emma Goldman.

Moritz writes, "To read 'Quibble with Hegel' you do not need any knowledge of the philosopher Hegel. If you don't have any, the title becomes an enigma, which I like. I can provide this: Hegel wrote a book of many hundreds of pages called *The Phenomenology of Spirit*. Some prefer *Mind*. Whichever, 'Quibble with Hegel,' though very short, is in fact the longer work. Hegel conveys the image of the oak tree and the acorn, just as the poem does, but he didn't manage to find space to include the monk and the children, the squirrels and the necklace, the blessing, the nibbling and the sleep, the hat and the currach, and the travelling-by-looking. Some will find this statement partly unfair to Hegel. Sometimes I do. Other times, not. Profound thanks to Mary Dalton, for her poetry above all."

MEGAN MORRISON lives on the unceded territories of the Coast Salish people, dividing her time between Pender Island and Vancouver. Her poems and stories have been awarded by *Grain*, *Room*, and *BTWN* magazines, as well as supported by the Writer's Trust Mentorship Program and the Canada Council for the Arts.

Morrison writes, "Like most poems, 'Some Questions' started surfacing before I really knew what was happening. It wasn't until I got the text down and could look at it, that I recognized it as a dog pile of anxieties. Some of these anxieties were familiar to me, others more distant and abstract. Yet they all seemed to belong to the same voice, the same moment in time. As I played around with the sentences, a character began to emerge. A woman at her sink, quietly ruminating. The scene in this poem feels very private to me. I think it's because of how the questions feel urgent, yet unspoken. Not even a question mark to validate them. I liked this woman, I knew her right away, and I wanted to untangle the quick rhythms of her thinking."

Montreal poet ERÍN MOURE has published more than fifty books since 1979, including poetry as well as poetry in translation by poets such as Nicole Brossard, Chantal Neveu and Fernando Pessoa, Chus Pato and Oana Avasilichioaei. She has received two Governor General's Awards, for poetry (1988) and for translation (2021), and holds two honorary doctorates (Vigo, Spain and Brandon, Manitoba, Canada).

Of "Flourish (May 2022)," Moure writes, "Written in spring 2022 for Mother's Day in Canada, the poem is a meditation on my own mom, by then long deceased, on what would have been our shared anguish over the Russian invasion and genocidal war on Ukraine, still ongoing today, and on us both, as indecent partisans of the snows whose job is hope and insistence on flourishing."

CASSANDRA MYERS (they/she/he) is a poet, illustrator, and dancer from Tkaronto, Ontario, but she would rather be living on a sailboat. Their poetry appears in *Arc Poetry Magazine*, *Canthius*, *Grain*, *Prairie Fire*, and has won a National Magazine Gold Award amongst others. They are currently on a sidequest in Thailand, and holding open calls for a new best friend.

Of "Squeal," Myers writes, "I wrote this poem after watching *Okja*, a film about a super pig who is a girl's best friend—until it's captured for meat. It includes the only depiction I've seen of sexual violence between animals with a clear dynamic of unnatural harm. While such violence is common in the animal world, we frame it biologically, not socially. If rape culture drives non-consensual acts in humans, what compels them in animals? And how do humans participate in this violence through farming and husbandry? The sonics of consent keep shifting. The pre-MeToo era I grew up in emphasized a clear, enthusiastic yes. As I heal from sexual violence and reclaim subtlety, bodily awareness, and non-verbal communication, I continue to risk my safety for the sake of relationships and desire—a gamble I wish none of us had to take. Gentleness is a sonic many of us have forgotten—or were never taught—to hear. I believe the full embodiment of gentleness is the highest purpose of human life, to love with delicacy, tenderness, and overcoming fear. I want to live in a world deeply attuned to subtlety, where every movement is precious, precise, and invited."

SHANE NEILSON is a poet and physician from New Brunswick. He will publish *The Reign*, a hybrid verse novel concerning the romance between a queer deer and an intellectually disabled man, with Goose Lane Editions in 2025. He served as co-judge of the International Hippocrates Poetry Prize this year.

Of "How to lose the audience," Neilson writes, "Let me tell you the backstory of this poem by way of its frontstory. On the day I received word of its acceptance from the Biblioasis team, I was scheduled to give a plenary talk in Miramichi, to an audience of physicians, on fostering non-neurotypical medical learners. The moment was full circle for me, discussing my difficult path through Dalhousie Medical School to the medical school itself so that people like me might have a better time of things going forward. Spurred mysteriously by the acceptance, I started off my talk by reading 'How to lose the audience' because it had New Brunswick in it (those chain-link fences by the ball diamond in Oromocto, shout out) but also because it was entirely reflective of the experiences I was trying to relate: being ill, psychotic, feeling great shame, all within medical spaces! Rarely in my life are things so meant to be, and receiving word of the inclusion of this poem was tremendously moving. Perhaps the poem will move in you too."

NOFEL is a Montreal-based poet and essayist whose work has appeared in various literary magazines. He was longlisted for the 2022 CBC Nonfiction Prize, and two of his poems were featured in *El Ghourabaa: A queer and trans collection of oddities* (Metonymy, 2024). He also contributed translations to *Arabic, between love and war* (trace, 2025).

Of "In Arabic," Nofel writes, "*Over the seabed, fish snivelled when the son left* is in reference to a traditional Iraqi song titled 'Rabaytak Zgayroun Hassan'; the line If you're in love, why deny it? is from the song 'Madam Teheb Betenker Leih' by Umm Kulthum (1898–1975). As a poet whose native language is Arabic, I endlessly tried writing poems in Arabic—to no avail. I think and feel in English, even in my dreams. I wanted to write a poem that captures my multilayered relationship with Arabic as an arabophone Canadian in Montreal, where Arabic lives vibrantly. I chose the ghazal form, which originated in Arabic and found its way to English, after passing through Persian and Urdu. I find it fascinating that the English ghazal maintained many of its Arabic poetic features such as the mono-rhyme before the refrain, although the refrain itself does not exist in Arabic. What makes me fond of the form in English is that it managed to appropriate a poetic form from my first language in a way that honours the allure of the Arabic original, rendering all and every ghazal a tribute to Arabic. Writing ghazals is my way of celebrating both my languages. This poem in particular is my love letter to Arabic, Montreal, Arab Montrealers, and Arabic speakers, wherever they may be. And, since English is the language in which I write my poems, every poem of mine is a love letter to English."

DAVID O'MEARA is the author of five collections of poetry, most recently *Masses on Radar* (Coach House Books). His novel, *Chandelier*, was published by Nightwood Editions in 2024. He is the current poet laureate (anglophone) of the City of Ottawa.

Of "Recess," O'Meara writes, "Last year, on a cold, wet, friendless autumn day I was passing a schoolyard flecked with puddles and fallen leaves. The bell rang for recess, that scheduled portion of afternoon designed to relieve us from study. I remember them mostly with dread. Each one contained all the anxieties of life in a pressure-cooker imposition of fun. It was terrifying."

JOHN O'NEILL lives in West Grey, Ontario. He has published poetry and fiction in numerous literary journals including *The Malahat Review*, *Prairie Fire*, CV2, EVENT, *The Dalhousie Review*, *Canadian Literature*, and *The New Quarterly*. His story collection *Goth Girls of Banff* (NeWest Press, 2020) was a finalist for a ReLit Award, the UBC/HarperCollins Prize for Best New Fiction, and for the Trade Fiction Book of the Year at the 2021 Alberta Book Publishing Awards. Every day (or most days anyway) he trundles off to a local café to work on his writing. He also hosts, with his artist wife Ann, a series of monthly "Art Salons" at the Durham Art Gallery.

Of "The News," O'Neill writes, "In 2022, my wife and I moved from Toronto to rural Ontario and this coincided with the Russian invasion of Ukraine. The reality of that catastrophe was heaped up on the stress of moving to an unfamiliar environment. My wife's parents were Ukrainian refugees from the Second World War. The first part of the poem came to me in the middle of the night, in our new forest home, and, as Bertrand Bickersteth observed in his comments on the poem (he chose it as first prize winner in the 2023 Prairie Fire/McNally Robinson poetry contest, a shout out to him), 'Here, the tragedy of the news is literally consumed in all its modern forms: radio, television, mobile devices.' There is no escape when information itself is a sort of poison—inevitably swallowed, potentially harming anyone, but especially those with a connection to a besieged country. There are many 'fronts' in a war. Civilization suddenly seems a facade, and the only way to survive is to become animal-like, to abandon reason, empathy, even language. In this abandonment, a marriage is threatened too, the narrator/husband tested by his wife's pain. These are some of the ideas/emotions I tried to capture in the poem."

MICHAEL ONDAATJE was born in Sri Lanka and lives in Toronto. He is the author of several award-winning novels, as well as a memoir, a nonfiction book on film, and several books of poetry including, most recently, *A Year of Last Things* (McClelland & Stewart, 2024). Among other accolades, his novel *The English Patient* won the Booker Prize, and *Anil's Ghost* won the *Irish Times* International Fiction Prize, the Giller prize, and the Prix Médicis.

CRAIG FRANCIS POWER is a writer and visual artist from St. John's, Newfoundland and Labrador. He is the author of four books, including *Total Party Kill* (Breakwater Books, 2024), a collection of poetry that explores addiction and sobriety through the imagery and vernacular of the table-top role-playing game Dungeons & Dragons.

Of "Walking My Three-Year-Old to Nanny's Place, Easter Sunday 2017," Power writes, "This poem—as the title suggests—was inspired by an experience I had walking my daughter through a part of St. John's where I'd once lived. I've found the experience of being a parent—not unlike the act of writing poetry itself—to be at times a baffling and daunting one: you just never know what will happen next, and only sometimes—if I'm paying enough attention—what happens next, as scary or painful or beautiful as it may be, helps me to see life, and myself, in a new way. God, how I suffered. I'm not joking one bit. But, trite as it sounds—trudging through that rough part of town with my head pounding—I'm glad I was conscious enough to hear my daughter's message and to get what was so obvious to her three-year-old self at that time. There's still so much to be grateful for."

JOHN REIBETANZ is happy to have lived in Toronto since 1968, during which time he completed twenty volumes of poetry. However, he is most proud of his three children and five grandchildren, all of whom enjoyed growing up in Toronto.

Of "Clams," Reibetanz writes, "'They were all as happy as clams in the little houses,' claimed the manager of the Standard Loan Company, determined to put a good face on his benevolence. But in this case, the language itself, as well as the circumstances of the 'actors' in his farce, dictated another outcome. And just as etymology assigned a different role to 'clams,' ('to cramp, fetter, constrict or pinch'), so the actual history of his people told a different story: of cold winds that carried whimpers of hungry children, of people sleeping on the floors of their kitchen to catch the warmth of their stove, or of passing trains 'picking off slower-moving children.' And finally, of clam shells scavenged from 'affluent garbage.'"

OZAYR SALOOJEE is a South African-Canadian writer, editor, and designer, teaching at Carleton University in Ottawa, where he is a professor of architecture and urbanism. His research and creative work explores writing as a spatial practice, of architecture enacted otherwise and of both of those as tender, epistemic dreaming and worlding.

Of "The Little Things," Saloojee writes, "I wrote this after seeing a dining-room-table amputation in a house in Gaza, in January 2024, a little less than three months into (a still on-going, as of this note's writing) genocide. I watched it on repeat—macabre, surreal—on a tiny screen. And it was the oh-so-simple and everyday familiar space and scene of that video that blurred the line between everything there and here, in Ottawa, with my own home and family and the spaces of our lives. The journalist and writer Omar El Akkad said that language is one of the structural supports of this particular slaughter, and so this text was a small attempt to grapple with the slipperiness that language affords, and the potential worlding—and maybe, just maybe—the liberation that language can help dream into being. I tried to write it 'with sharper teeth' (as Fargo Tbakhi speaks of the craft of writing during the hour of genocide), but also to balance it with a tenderness worthy of those who cared for Ahed, the young woman in that grainy video. For what little it's worth—this work is dedicated to the Bseiso family."

VIVEK SHARMA was born in a small village in the foothills of the Himalayas and now resides in the unceded territory of the Syilx/Okanagan peoples. Author of *Between Two Valleys, A Lake* (Anstruther Press, 2025), Sharma has published work in various Canadian magazines including *Arc Poetry*, *The Fiddlehead*, *The Malahat Review*, *Prairie Fire*, and elsewhere.

Sharma writes, "'Imaginary Breakfast with Real People' is the first poem I wrote after coming to Canada. As with my other poems, it came out of a real-life experience, an *encounter*, of the dramatic monologue kind, with a chatty interlocutor (my Iraqi roommate) in a one-sided conversation with the silent speaker. Jet-lagged and dazed, the *I/eye* struggles to adjust to a new place—a domestic space both familiar and strange, and the mind wanders, imagining what's lost: rivers and mountains, wide open expanse of it all. But the roommate's words pull the *speaker* back to the apartment, the shared kitchen. In her essay, 'Some Notes toward a Poetics,' Lyn Hejinian writes: 'A poetics gets formed in and as a relationship with the world.' As an outsider writing about diaspora and Canada, I question my relationship with the world—the way I see and understand things 'launched in context' and in 'the space of appearance,' such as the encounter where the speaker comes face to face with a singular happening, 'a clogged sink [. . .] slowly suffocating in a sludge / of leftovers.' Both singularity and commonality become the same occurrence, to paraphrase Hejinian, a mediating ground for the reader where poetry survives."

SUE SINCLAIR grew up in Newfoundland on Beothuk territory, and she is the author of six collections of poetry, including her latest book, *Almost Beauty: New and Selected Poems* (Goose Lane Editions, 2022). Another collection, *New-Fangled Rose*, will appear in spring 2026 with Goose Lane Editions. All of Sue's books have won or been nominated for a variety of awards. She teaches creative writing at the University of New Brunswick on Wolastoqiyik territory.

Of "Pfeilstorch," Sinclair writes, "I wish I could remember where I first heard about Pfeilstorchs. The poem is one of those straightforward cases when you (I) come across a feature of the world that is so strange and enigmatic that a poem comes pouring out of you (me). The Pfeilstorch confirms for me that poetry is in the world; it's not something I make up but something I channel. The worry always is, of course, whether I can create a poem that lives up to the compelling phenomenon I'm hoping to address. But if I worried too much about that, I'd never write a thing. I may have come across the Pfeilstorch when reading about bird migration ... I regret that this part of these cyborg-birds' incredible story didn't make it into the poem; when I tried, the exposition took over from the poetry. But now's my chance: it wasn't always known that storks and other birds in the northern hemisphere fly south in the winter. There were other theories about their disappearance, including that they hibernated. Finding birds in Europe with African spears embedded in their bodies proved that they had indeed been south."

KAREN SOLIE was born in Moose Jaw and grew up in southwest Saskatchewan. Her most recent collection is *Wellwater* (Anansi, Picador, 2025; FSG, 2026).

Of "Prime Location," Solie writes, "To live with housing precarity is to be hyper-aware of dwellings, of their life cycles in the city's ecosystem and of the values that create that ecosystem. Dwellings are also prime locations for nostalgia, as are poems themselves."

MISHA SOLOMON is a homosexual poet in and of Tiohtià:ke/Montreal. He is the author of two chapbooks and his work has appeared in *Arc Poetry Magazine*, *Best Canadian Poetry 2024*, *CV2*, *The Fiddlehead*, *Geist*, *Grain*, *The Malahat Review*, and *Riddle Fence*. His full-length debut collection, *My Great-Grandfather Danced Ballet*, is forthcoming with Brick Books in 2026.

Solomon writes, "I wrote 'Yoo-Hoo' while participating in Sage Hill's Emerging Writers' Course, in response to a prompt from the incredible poet and teacher Lisa Richter. The prompt was itself based on 'You Are Who I Love' by Aracelis Girmay. 'Yoo-Hoo,' which began as a play on the repeated 'you' and 'who' in Girmay's poem, is an attempt to explore desires for attention and recognition, and to grapple with feeling somewhat unseen, as I felt before I began to actively pursue writing and publishing poetry. In thinking about the origins of the poem, I am particularly struck by the webs of connection provided by a creative life: I originally met Lisa in a poetry studio given by Sarah Burgoyne (during which I wrote the poem that was selected for *BCP 2024*) and I was profoundly inspired by Lisa's *Nautilus and Bone* while writing *My Great-Grandfather Danced Ballet*."

SUSAN WHITE (she/her) lives in St. John's, Newfoundland and Labrador, a province that is the traditional homeland of diverse Indigenous peoples. She has a background in journalism and currently works in communications. She's also a master of arts in creative writing candidate at Memorial University. Her poetry has been featured in *Riddle Fence*, *Horseshoe Literary Magazine*, and *Paragon*.

Of "Some Late for Them to Be at the Fish," White writes, "This poem focuses on a quiet, intimate moment with my grandmother in the days before she died of cancer. My parents, with support from my aunts, cared for her for as long as possible in their home. We used to sit by her bedside, keeping her company, as her mind wandered along morphine-guided paths. There was a photograph on the wall of my grandfather's fishing premises, called 'rooms' or a 'stage' in Newfoundland vernacular, and it seemed to send her back to a time when Pop still fished, the cod were plentiful, and she would watch the stage from her kitchen window to see if he was walking up the road for supper. I felt I had little option but to join her in that time."

ERIN WILSON is from the rural north. Her poems have appeared in *The Fiddlehead*, *Grain*, *Prairie Fire*, EVENT, *FreeFall*, *The Antigonish Review*, *The Dalhousie Review*, *Queen's Quarterly*, *Vallum*, and elsewhere internationally. Poems from her second collection, *Blue* (Circling Rivers, 2022), were longlisted for the CBC Poetry Prize. She's won a Pushcart. She lives on Robinson-Huron Treaty Territory. She's happiest in the woods.

Of "Ode to Joy," Wilson writes, "I had an old radio in my kitchen. Good things came through that radio. I'm a CBC girl. I learned philosophy, history, art, music, literature. It was joy. But the terror of news also found me: homelessness, poverty, climate change, the pandemic, Russia's invasion of Ukraine, the war in Gaza. No matter where the news happens, it's happening to us. Any strike against a human is a strike against every human. So, in order to stay sane in the temple of my own life, I turned off the radio. First days of the pandemic, I bought a record player. Playing albums reconnected me. I'd play Beethoven's 'Ode to Joy' while cooking. My simple surroundings blessed me. This poem, in return, was my gratitude. Later, I'd encounter a video of Leonard Bernstein introducing the *Ninth*. He said, '...to all these people, to all classes, nationalities and racial backgrounds, this music speaks a universality of thought, of human brotherhood, of freedom and love ... In this time of world agony and hopelessness and helplessness, we love his music and we need it. As despairing as we may be, we can not listen to this *Ninth Symphony* without emerging from it changed, enriched, encouraged ...'"

JAEYUN YOO is a Korean-Canadian poet and psychiatrist living on the unceded territories of the Musqueam, Squamish, and Tsleil-Waututh peoples, also known as Vancouver. Her poems have appeared in various literary magazines and anthologies including *Best Canadian Poetry 2025*. She won *The Fiddlehead*'s 2023 Ralph Gustafson Poetry Prize. Her first solo chapbook is forthcoming with Baseline Press in 2026.

Of "have you seen my father," Yoo writes, "This poem started from a place of love and grief, but in the process of writing and revising, it became a broader reflection about the sociocultural experiences of immigrant families."

PATRICIA YOUNG was born and still lives in Victoria, British Columbia. She has published fourteen collections of poetry, the most recent, *Amateurs at Love* (2018), with Goose Lane Editions. She has been nominated twice for the Governor General's Award, won the Pat Lowther Memorial Award, and twice won the BC

Book Poetry Prize. She won the inaugural Metcalf-Rooke Award for her collection of short fiction, *Airstream* (Biblioasis, 2011).

Of "The Thing with the Wings," Young writes, "Through our adult children, my husband and I have become acquainted with dogs. This poem evolved out of dog-sitting Fozzy Bear, our son and daughter-in-law's rescue terrier-poodle mix, found on the streets of California and brought to Edmonton by an adoption agency. In the end, the poem is not really about Fozz (who despite being very sweet does bark at school children walking past the house) but about some kind of creature or force entering one's life and changing it dramatically."

NOTABLE POEMS

KC Adams, "A Diptych," *Prairie Fire* 45.3

Katherine Barbour, "She asks me how I'm doing," *untethered* 15

Dominique Bernier-Cormier, "Anything Other Than Itself," *The Malahat Review* 226

Brandi Bird, "What Do People Do at Night?" *Contemporary Verse 2* 46.3

Dylan Clark, "Key Cutting Machine," *Arc Poetry Magazine* 104

Marlene Cookshaw, "The Life Separate," *The Malahat Review* 225

Zachary Cooper, "Dear Alex:," *Contemporary Verse 2* 46.4

Sue Croll, "Fetish," *The Fiddlehead* 301

Phillip Crymble, "Omega Man," *The Ampersand Review* 5

Robert Currie, "Trying to Get Home," *Grain* 51.2

Lynn Davies, "Shelling Peas," *Literary Review of Canada* September 2024

Don Domanski, "Nocturne of Birth and Water," *EVENT* 53.1

Guy Elston, "The Work," *The Ex-Puritan* 66/67

Tarini Fernando, "the distraction," *filling Station* 83

Neil Griffin, "Youghal Mudlands," *EVENT* 53.2

Harold Hoefle, "Cross Country Runner," *FreeFall* 34.1

Danielle Hubbard, "Why my mother loved reusable bags," *Room* 47.4

Liz Huntly, "lawn mower," *Room* 47.4

Meghan Kemp-Gee, "Deep Cove Is Six Miles Away," *Grain* 51.3

Sarah Klassen, "bus shelter," *Prairie Fire* 45.3

Aaron Kreuter, "Good Mood Fleeting," *Arc Poetry Magazine* 104

Cory Lavender, "Colleen McGee on Hard Times," *Grain* 51.3

Ana Rodriguez Machado, "Did you forget anything?," *Contemporary Verse 2* 46.4

Annie MacKillican, "Revolution headquarters," *The Malahat Review* 228

Diana Manole, "Mom's Cravings in Her Old Age: Mom's getting better at distinguishing real from unreal," *subTerrain* 97

Katie Martí, "Things for Which I Grieve," *Room* 46.4

David Martin, "Rhyme Decay," *FreeFall* 34.1

Sadie McCarney, "Swansong," *EVENT* 53.1

Marco Melfi, "Safeway Bags Play Hooky," *The New Quarterly* 171

Cara-Lyn Morgan, "What Do I Know of This Mother Tongue?," *Geist* 126

Susan Musgrave, "A Condition Incompatible with Life," *Border Crossings* 164

Meredith Quartermain, "A Miraculous Platter," *The Malahat Review* 226

kerry rawlinson, "St. Helens as a Metaphor for Everything," *Grain* 52.1

Rebekah Rempel, "Crown-of-Thorns Starfish," *Canthius* 13

Shane Rhodes, "It's Here All The Beauty I Told You About," *The New Quarterly* 169

Natalie Rice, "Common Herbs, Shrubs, and Mosses of Nova Scotia," *Queen's Quarterly* 131.3

Andrea Scott, "Prepping the Beds," *The New Quarterly* 171

Tosh Sherkat, "Who Doesn't Want Anything," *Grain* 51.4

Carolyn Smart, "Sick to death," *The New Quarterly* 170

Sue Sorensen, "And One for Bob," *The Malahat Review* 225

Joanna Streetly, "Fire Behaviour," *Prairie Fire* 45.1

Paula Turcotte, "Spoiler alert: nobody in this poem wins," *Contemporary Verse 2* 46.4

Chimwemwe Undi, "Winnipeg Poem," *Geist* 127

Paul Vermeersch, "We Have Learned to See Camouflage as Conspicuous," *Riddle Fence* 53

Rob Winger, "Reverse Imaginary Time Capsule," *The Ampersand Review* 5

Sarah Wolfson, "On Breaking," *Arc Poetry Magazine* 104

Christine Wu, "The Countdown," *Grain* 51.4

Meryem Yildiz, "What You Do Not Know Yet," *Arc Poetry Magazine* 105

Terence Young, "Understudy," *EVENT* 52.3

Zico, "World on Fire," *Arc Poetry Magazine* 105

MAGAZINES CONSULTED

Each year, the fifty best poems and the list of notable poems by Canadian poets are selected from more than fifty print and online journals published in the previous year. While direct submissions of individual poems are not accepted, we welcome review copies from print outlets and announcements of new issues from online publications. Please direct two copies of each print issue to Best Canadian Poetry c/o Biblioasis, 1686 Ottawa St., Ste 100, Windsor, ON N8Y 1R1, or email us at bestcanadian@biblioasis.com.

The Adroit Journal (theadroitjournal.org)

Ahoy (ahoyliterary.github.io)

The Ampersand Review (theampersandreview.ca). Sheridan College, Hazel McCallion Campus, Room B580, 4180 Duke of York Blvd., Mississauga, ON L5B 0G5

The Antigonish Review (antigonishreview.com). PO Box 5000, Antigonish, NS, B2G 2W5

Arc Poetry Magazine (arcpoetry.ca). PO Box 81060, Ottawa, ON, K1P 1B1

Border Crossings (bordercrossingsmag.com)

Brick, A Literary Journal (brickmag.com). PO Box 609, Stn. P, Toronto, ON, M5S 2Y4

Bywords (bywords.ca)

Canadian Literature (canlit.ca). University of British Columbia, Mary Bollert Hall, Room 111, 6253 NW Marine Drive, Vancouver, BC, V6T 1Z1

Canthius (canthius.com)

The Capilano Review (thecapilanoreview.ca). 102–281 Industrial Ave., Vancouver, BC, V6A 2P2

carte blanche (carte-blanche.org)

Columba Poetry (columbapoetry.com)

Common House Magazine (commonhousemag.com)

Contemporary Verse 2 (CV2) (contemporaryverse2.ca). 502–100 Arthur St., Winnipeg, MB, R3B 1H3

The Dalhousie Review (ojs.library.dal.ca/dalhousiereview). Dalhousie University, Halifax, NS, B3H 4R2

EVENT (eventmagazine.ca). PO Box 2503, New Westminster, BC, V3L 5B2

The Ex-Puritan (ex-puritan.ca)

The Fiddlehead (thefiddlehead.ca). Campus House, University of New Brunswick, 11 Garland Ct., PO Box 4400, Fredericton, NB, E3B 5A3

filling Station (fillingstation.ca). PO Box 22135, Bankers Hall, Calgary, AB, T2P 4J5

FreeFall (freefallmagazine.ca). 250 Maunsell Close, NE Calgary, AB T2E 7C2

Funicular Magazine (funicularmagazine.com)

Geist (geist.com). Suite 210, 111 W. Hastings St., Vancouver, BC, V6B 1H4

Grain (grainmagazine.ca). PO Box 3986, Regina, SK, S4P 3R9

Granta (granta.com)

HA&L (*Hamilton Arts & Letters*) (halmagazine.wordpress.com)

Horseshoe Literary Magazine (horseshoejournal.ca)

Janus Unbound (janusunbound.com). Memorial University of Newfoundland and Labrador, 230 Elizabeth Ave, St. John's, NL A1C 5S7

Juniper (juniperpoetry.com)

Literary Review of Canada (reviewcanada.ca). 340 King St. E., Toronto, ON, M5A 1K8

Maisonneuve (maisonneuve.org). 1051 boul. Decarie, PO Box 53527, Saint Laurent, QC, H4L 5J9

The Malahat Review (malahatreview.ca). University of Victoria, PO Box 1700, Stn. CSC, Victoria, BC, V8W 2Y2

The Nashwaak Review (stu.ca/english/the-nashwaak-review). St. Thomas University, Fredericton, NB, E3B 5G3

The New Quarterly (tnq.ca). St. Jerome's University, 290 Westmount Rd. N., Waterloo, ON, N2L 3G3

Newfoundland Quarterly (nqonline.ca). Memorial University of Newfoundland, Signal Hill Campus, 100 Signal Hill Rd., St. John's, NL, A1C 5S7

Parentheses (parenthesesjournal.com)

Periodicities (periodicityjournal.blogspot.com)

Pinhole Poetry (pinholepoetry.ca)

Plenitude Magazine (plenitudemagazine.ca)

Poetry Pause (poets.ca/poetrypause)

Prairie Fire (prairiefire.ca). 423–100 Arthur St., Winnipeg, MB, R3B 1H3

PRISM *international* (prismmagazine.ca). Creative Writing Program, University of British Columbia, Buchanan Room E462, 1866 Main Mall, Vancouver, BC, V6T 1Z1

Queen's Quarterly (queensu.ca/quarterly). Queen's University, 144 Barrie St., Kingston, ON, K7L 3N6

Qwerty (qwertyunb.com). University of New Brunswick Department of English, P.O. Box 4400, 19 Macaulay Lane, Fredericton, NB, E3B 5A3

Ricepaper Magazine (ricepapermagazine.ca). PO Box 74174, Hillcrest RPO, Vancouver, BC, V5V 5L8

Riddle Fence (riddlefence.com)

Room (roommagazine.com). PO Box 46160, Stn. D, Vancouver, BC, V6J 5G5

Rust & Moth (rustandmoth.com)

subTerrain (subterrain.ca). PO Box 3008, MPO,
Vancouver, BC, V6B 3X5

Talking About Strawberries (talkingaboutstrawberries.blogspot.com)

The /tƐmz/ Review (thetemzreview.com)

The Times Literary Supplement (the-tls.co.uk).
1 London Bridge Street, London SE1 9GF

Touch the Donkey (touchthedonkey.blogspot.com)

The Typescript (thetypescript.com)

untethered (alwaysuntethered.com)

Verdant (verdantjournal.ca)

The Walrus (walrusmagazine.com).
411 Richmond St. E., Suite B15, Toronto, ON, M5A 3S5

yolk (yolkliterary.ca)

INDEX TO POETS

ACKNOWLEDGEMENTS

"Checkpoint of the Mouth" first appeared in *Queen's Quarterly* copyright © Ronna Bloom. Reprinted with permission of the author.

"Clams" first appeared in *The Fiddlehead* copyright © John Reibetanz. Reprinted with permission of the author.

"Criseyde" first appeared in the *Times Literary Supplement* copyright © Irina Dumitrescu. Reprinted with permission of the author.

"Cursing, Flailing" appeared in *Geist* copyright © Evelyn Lau. Reprinted from *Parade of Storms* by Evelyn Lau (Anvil Press, 2025) with permission of the author and publisher.

"Darwin Awards Song" first appeared in *EVENT* copyright © John Wall Barger. Reprinted with permission of the author.

"Fancy University Boy" appeared in *The Fiddlehead* copyright © Conor Kerr. Reprinted from *Beaver Hills Forever* by Conor Kerr (Arsenal Pulp Press, 2025) with permission of the author and publisher.

"Flourish (May 2022)" first appeared in *carte blanche* copyright © Erín Moure. Reprinted with permission of the author.

"Gay Messiah" appeared in *EVENT* copyright © Estlin McPhee. Reprinted from *In Your Nature* by Estlin McPhee (Brick Books, 2025) with permission of the author and publisher.

"have you seen my father" first appeared in *The Fiddlehead* copyright © Jaeyun Yoo. Reprinted with permission of the author.

"How to lose the audience" first appeared in *The Malahat Review* copyright © Shane Neilson. Reprinted with permission of the author.

"How To Pack for Internment (150 Pounds)" first appeared in *The New Quarterly* copyright © Kevin Irie. Reprinted with permission of the author.

"Imaginary Breakfast with Real People" appeared in *The Fiddlehead* copyright © Vivek Sharma. Reprinted from *Between Two Valleys, a Lake* by Vivek Sharma (Anstruther Press, 2025) with permission of the author and publisher.

"In Arabic" first appeared in *Geist* copyright © Nofel. Reprinted with permission of the author.

"In the Wake of" first appeared in *Granta* copyright © Sylvia Legris. Reprinted with permission of the author.

"It Is Not Heart to Essay" first appeared in *The Malahat Review* copyright © Glenn Hayes. Reprinted with permission of the author.

"Lending Library, Heaven" appeared in *Geist* copyright © Danielle Devereaux. Reprinted from *The Chrome Chair* by Danielle Devereaux (Riddle Fence Publishing, 2024) with permission of the author and publisher.

"The Little Things" first appeared in *Janus Unbound* copyright © Ozayr Saloojee. Reprinted with permission of the author.

"Local Fishermen" first appeared in *Queen's Quarterly* copyright © George Moore. Reprinted with permission of the author.

"Lock" from *A Year of Last Things: Poems* by Michael Ondaatje, copyright © 2024 by Michael Ondaatje. Reprinted by permission of McClelland & Stewart, a division of Penguin Random House Canada Limited, and Alfred A. Knopf, an imprint of the Knopf Doubleday Publishing Group, a division of Penguin Random House LLC. All rights reserved. Any third party use of this material, outside of this publication, is prohibited. Interested parties must apply directly to Penguin Random House Canada Limited for permission. Selected from *The Walrus*.

"Looking for Something Written, the Ideal Reader" first appeared in *subTerrain* copyright © M. W. Miller. Reprinted with permission of the author.

"Lucky" first appeared in *The Fiddlehead* copyright © Puneet Dutt. Reprinted with permission of the author.

"from *Monoculture: A commentary of monologues*" appeared in *Riddle Fence* copyright © Sue Goyette. Reprinted from *Monoculture* by Sue Goyette (Gaspereau Press, 2022) with permission of the author and publisher.

“A mudlarker’s diary” first appeared in *subTerrain* copyright © Ariel Gordon. Reprinted with permission of the author.

“My answer to the question ‘how are you?’ at the grocery store” first appeared in *Contemporary Verse 2* copyright © Petra Chambers. Reprinted with permission of the author.

“The News” first appeared in *Prairie Fire* copyright © John O’Neill. Reprinted with permission of the author.

“Nôhkom” first appeared in *FreeFall* copyright © Jennifer Gossoo. Reprinted with permission of the author.

“Ode to Joy” first appeared in *Queen’s Quarterly* copyright © Erin Wilson. Reprinted with permission of the author.

“On the Use of the Sextant” first appeared in *The Walrus* copyright © Richard Greene. Reprinted with permission of the author.

“Painkiller” from *Midway* copyright © 2024 by Kayla Czaga. Reproduced with permission from House of Anansi Press, Toronto. www.houseofanansi.com. Appeared in *Room* copyright © Kayla Czaga.

“Pfeilstorch” first appeared in *Riddle Fence* copyright © Sue Sinclair. Reprinted with permission of the author.

“Prime Location” from *Wellwater* copyright © 2025 by Karen Solie. Reproduced with permission from House of Anansi Press, Toronto. www.houseofanansi.com. Appeared in *The Walrus* copyright © Karen Solie.

“Quibble with Hegel” from *Great Silent Ballad* copyright © 2024 by A. F. Moritz. Reproduced with permission from

House of Anansi Press, Toronto. www.houseofanansi.com. Appeared in *The Malahat Review* copyright © A. F. Moritz.

"Real Estate Sign" first appeared in *The Malahat Review* copyright © Dave Hickey. Reprinted with permission of the author.

"Recess" first appeared in *The Walrus* copyright © David O'Meara. Reprinted with permission of the author.

"Requirement Galore" first appeared in *Horseshoe* copyright © Paul Moorehead. Reprinted with permission of the author.

"The Science of Skipping Stones" first appeared in *EVENT* copyright © Steve McOrmond. Reprinted with permission of the author.

"Some Late for Them to Be at the Fish" first appeared in *Riddle Fence* copyright © Susan White. Reprinted with permission of the author.

"Some Questions" first appeared in *Grain* copyright © Megan Morrison. Reprinted with permission of the author.

"Squeal" first appeared in *The Malahat Review* copyright © Cassandra Myers. Reprinted with permission of the author.

"Storytelling for Young Warriors" first appeared in *EVENT* copyright © Henry Heavyshield. Reprinted with permission of the author.

"Surfacing, Copenhagen Harbour" first appeared in *Prairie Fire* copyright © Carolina Corcoran. Reprinted with permission of the author.

“That’s Not a Piñata, That’s a Hornets’ Nest” appeared in *The Nashwaak Review* and *Queen’s Quarterly* copyright © Darrell Epp. Reprinted with permission of the author.

“The Thing with the Wings” first appeared in *The Dalhousie Review* copyright © Patricia Young. Reprinted with permission of the author.

“To the Border Agent Who Confiscated My Book of Poetry” first appeared in *Grain* copyright © Nicholas Bradley. Reprinted with permission of the author.

“Uber-Eats Ghazal” first appeared in *EVENT* copyright © Khashayar “Kess” Mohammadi. Reprinted with permission of the author.

“Walking My Three-Year-Old to Nanny’s Place, Easter Sunday 2017” first appeared in *The Malahat Review* copyright © Craig Francis Power. Reprinted with permission of the author.

“We’re Doubling Down, Say Darren Woods” first appeared in *Prairie Fire* copyright © Nancy Huggett. Reprinted with permission of the author.

“What I Learned from Living Abroad” appeared in *The New Quarterly* copyright © Susan Glickman. Reprinted from *Cathedral/Grove* by Susan Glickman (Signal Editions, 2023) with permission of the author and publisher.

“Yellow Felt Stars” first appeared in *The Malahat Review* copyright © Emily Kedar. Reprinted with permission of the author.

“Yoo-Hoo” first appeared in *Riddle Fence* copyright © Misha Solomon. Reprinted with permission of the author.

EDITORS' BIOGRAPHIES

MARY DALTON is the author of six books of poetry, among them *Merrybegot*, *Red Ledger*, *Hooking*, and *Interrobang*, as well as a prose miscellany, *Edge: Essays, Reviews, Interviews.* The book version of her 2020 Pratt Lecture, *The Vernacular Strain in Newfoundland Poetry*, was released by Breakwater in 2022. She lives in St. John's, Newfoundland.

ANITA LAHEY's third poetry collection, *While Supplies Last*, was published by Véhicule Press in 2023. She's also co-author of the graphic-novel-in-verse, *Fire Monster*, a collaboration with artist Pauline Conley (Palimpsest, 2023). Her memoir *The Last Goldfish: a True Tale of Friendship* was a finalist for the 2021 Ottawa Book Award. Anita first joined *Best Canadian Poetry* as assistant series editor in 2014, and has served as series editor since 2018. She lives with her family in Ottawa.